"Chase your dream and make your life an adventure."
-Ruben Gonzalez

Ruben Gonzalez
Salt Lake City Olympics 84 MPH

The Courage To Succeed

Success Secrets of an
Unlikely
Four-Time Olympian

by
Ruben Gonzalez

Olympia Press

What other top achievers are saying about Ruben Gonzalez and "The Courage to Succeed"

"Adventure, determination, danger, perseverance – this is one unbelievable success story. Ruben Gonzalez achieved what few people ever do - mastery of his will. Motivating and inspiring!"

Dr. Stephen Covey
Author of *The 7 Habits of Highly Effective People*

"*The Courage to Succeed* is filled with excellent advice. Apply its teachings and watch your life change."

Ken Blanchard
Coauthor of *The One Minute Manager*

"*The Courage to Succeed* is truly an encouraging work. You will be motivated and inspired to embark on a journey that will take you further than you ever dreamed. Read it carefully, follow the plan that Ruben lays out for you, and you will have a life-changing experience."

Zig Ziglar
Legendary Motivational Speaker and Teacher
Author of *See You at the Top*

"I was there for the Miracle on Ice in Lake Placid in 1980 and, again, for the miracle on the mountain in Utah in 2002. No Olympian I have ever met has more of what makes a champion than Ruben Gonzalez. Read and internalize, and you will realize and materialize your own dreams."

Dr. Denis Waitley
Author of *Seeds of Greatness*
Former Chairman of Psychology, US Olympic Committee's Sports Medicine Council

"If you will read *The Courage to Succeed* or listen to Ruben speak, your life will change for the positive."

Lou Holtz
Legendary Notre Dame Football Coach
Author of *Winning Every Day*

"Ruben teaches us that once we transform our fear into energy we begin to transform our dreams into reality."

Gerhard Gschwandtner
Founder and Publisher, *Selling Power Magazine*

"Ruben's not only earned his spurs, but he's for real. His thankful spirit and his humble attitude, makes him one of the most wonderful speakers, most genuine speakers I have heard in my life and I recommend him with all my heart to you."

Charlie "Tremendous" Jones
Author of *Life is Tremendous*

"Ruben Gonzalez' exciting story of hard work, dedication and commitment – leading to success and achievement in the greatest competition in the world – is inspiring and uplifting in a wonderful way."

Brian Tracy
Author of *Million Dollar Habits*

"Ruben is a testament to the power of the human spirit. His book is a passionate call to action, challenging you to be the best that you can be. Through his amazing Olympic story, Ruben will inspire you to pursue your dream, equip you to get through the struggle and encourage you on to victory."

Rudy Ruettiger
Inspiration for the blockbuster movie, *Rudy*

"Inspirational. Ruben has a unique ability to motivate and challenge his audiences. His compelling story about triumph over adversity on the road to the Olympics provokes us all to set and reach lofty goals."

Jack Canfield
Author of *The Success Principles*

"Practical advice that will energize and empower you to succeed. Ruben hits you with the absolute truth about what it takes to succeed in the real world."

Jim Rohn
America's Foremost Business Philosopher

"Ruben's message of determination, commitment and persistence struck home with our sales organization. His inspirational message proves he is a winner not only in the greatest sporting competition of all, but also in team motivation. He is living testament to the concept of 'Never Quit!'"

Jerry Farmer
VP North American Sales Xerox

"*The Courage to Succeed* captures the spirit of the Olympics and reaffirms the invincibility of the human spirit."

Dr. Robert Schuller
Founder of the Crystal Cathedral
Author of *Move Ahead with Possibility Thinking*
Host of *The Hour of Power*

"Both Success and Failure exact a great price. If you search for success, this could be the ultimate document for your journey. Ruben paid an enormous price for his Olympic lessons. His life is an enviable one today. Yours can be as well. This is your roadmap!"

Ty Boyd
Founder of Executive Learning Systems,
Past President of the National Speakers
Association

"You will never be the same after reading *The Courage to Succeed*. It's powerful."

Pat Williams
Senior Vice President Orlando Magic

"From the corporate sales standpoint, Ruben's story and his recipe for success is a must read for any sales leader."

Ces Guerra
Sales Manager AstraZeneca Pharmaceuticals

"Ruben knows the steps to success. His enthusiasm and positive attitude are contagious!"

Mark Victor Hansen
Co-creator of *Chicken Soup for the Soul*

"Ruben Gonzalez is on a mission to see others succeed. Success does leave clues and Ruben has been on a life long search with a magnifying glass in one hand and a torch in the other hand. Ruben is inviting us along with him to blaze a trail of success and legacy."

George A. Palombo
Executive Director - American Center for Character and Cultural Education, 2001 Pennsylvania Police Officer of The Year

"Terrific! Ruben is a true Rhino! His crystal-clear vision of success cuts through all boundaries. *The Courage to Succeed* challenges us to do more, be more, take more chances, and ultimately live life to the max."

Scott Alexander
Author of *Rhinoceros Success*

"Ruben Gonzalez' life confirms an age old truth; determination, faith and believing in your God given abilities are still some of the keys to personal success."

Wally Amos
Author of *The Cookie Never Crumbles*

"I don't know when I have ever enjoyed reading such an exciting story about any one individual in all of my life. Reading Ruben's story inspires me to seek to get in the game of life and not simply stay on the sidelines. This book will inspire you to do the same."

Dr. Robert A. Rohm
President of Personality Insights, Inc
Author of *Positive Personality Profiles*

The Courage to Succeed
(Vancouver Edition)
By Ruben Gonzalez

ISBN -10: 0975554719
ISBN - 13: 978-0-9755547-1-5

Published by Olympia Press
832-689-8282

The #1 question people ask me after listening to my speeches is:

"How can I be more successful and get better results in everything I do?"

This book is the answer to that question.

Congratulations

You've just taken a step towards making your dreams a reality. Most people wish about their dreams and talk about their dreams, but they don't act on their dreams. The simple fact that you are investing in yourself shows you are doing something to get you closer to your dream.

Zig Ziglar said that you have to be before you can do and you have to do before you can have. By investing in yourself you are becoming more capable of reaching your dream. You're stacking the odds in your favor.

This Book Could Change Your Life
(But only if you apply its information)

Following these five tips will help you turn the information in this book into habits that will change your life:

1. **Read this book more than once.** I've read both "*Think and Grow Rich*" and "*The Magic of Thinking Big*" every year for the last 20 years. The more times you read a book, the more you become like the book.

2. **Underline and make notes.** Make sure you have a pen and highlighter in hand. Underlining specific lines and paragraphs will triple your retention rate. Write your own thoughts in the margins and own this book.

3. **Re-read your underlines.** Re-read your key items over and over. Record and listen to your notes.

4. **Apply the material immediately.** Doing so will help you understand the material better. Don't try to be perfect. Done is better than perfect.

5. **Prioritize what you want to learn.** Select one to three things from the book, apply them faithfully and make them a habit.

Acknowledgements

Thank you for your time, encouragement, and help.

My wife, Cheryl; my parents Ruben and Gloliley Gonzalez; my brother, Marcelo Gonzalez; my in-laws, Bob and Laurell Cunningham; Jeanne Cunningham, Dmitry Feld, George Tucker, Gunther Lemmerer, Tom Duffy, Christian Atance, Jonathan Edwards, Ken Anderson, Robert Taleanu, Joe Heller, Jim Jacobus, Pete Hinojosa, Greg Reid, Jon Owen, Jose Feliciano, Todd Guest, Craig Wear, Pablo Garcia, Todd Elgie, Don Akers, Garrison Wynn, Rick Mock, Mitch Peairson, Austin Davis, Shiva Keshavan, Tony Benshoof, Werner Hoeger, Claudio Atance, Ron Summers, Domen Pociecha, Fred Zimny, Nodar Kumaritashvili, David Corbin, Gail Stolzenberg, Adam Cook, Patrick Singleton, Grega Hacin, Bogdan Macovei, Mark Grimmette, Ricardo Raschini, Ioan Apostol, Paul Hildgartner, Carlos Quiroz, Walter Corey, Heather Schue, Rich Kolko, Mike Swartztrauber, Frank Masley, Duncan Kennedy, Keen Van Ditmar, Dr. David Calvo, Bengt Walden, and many more...

This book is dedicated to everyone who ever had a dream and had the guts to go after it.

"Ask not alone for victory. Ask for courage. For if you can endure, you bring honor to yourself, even more, you bring honor to us all."

- Unknown

Contents

Part 1 – Against All Odds

Part 2 – How to Become Unstoppable

Part 3 – Stories That Will Help You Win

Part 4 - From Rags to Riches

Appendix

Introduction by Zig Ziglar

Ruben Gonzalez is an inspired speaker and author. This book, *The Courage to Succeed*, will inspire you to get serious about commitment, responsibility, and direction in your life.

In it, Ruben uses his amazing Olympic experiences to encourage and direct you, the reader, as to how to make and keep commitments as you reach for your objectives.

I believe you will become caught up in his enthusiasm and persuasive assurances. Read it carefully, take it seriously, and follow through—and I really will *See You at the Top*.

Zig Ziglar
Author and Motivational Teacher

Foreword by Lou Holtz

Ruben Gonzalez in an ordinary person who got to compete in four Olympic games in spite of always being the last kid picked to play sports in school and in spite of not taking up his Olympic sport - the luge, until he was 21 years old.

He did it by consistently and persistently following a set of success principles that will work for anyone, anywhere, anytime. He shares those principles in this book.

Ruben is an outstanding, accomplished and inspiring keynote speaker. His timeless message is applicable to anyone who is dedicated and committed to improving their performance and achieving their goals and dreams.

More than just a motivator, Ruben's story is an inspiration to anyone who is going through struggles and has thought about quitting the pursuit of their dreams.

Ruben has written a book that you will love. In it, he shares the principles he used to realize his Olympic dream. I believe that as you read Ruben's common sense ideas, you will think he's right there, by your side, sharing his insights, pointing you up the right path. *The Courage to Succeed* is more than just a book; it's a blueprint to success.

Ruben will help you identify your dream. Then, he'll help you discover your strengths. Finally, he'll be by your side as you use those strengths to realize your dreams. *The Courage to Succeed* does more than tell Ruben's personal views on success. Ruben will get you to see that reaching your dream is possible, and then he'll inspire you and equip you to take the necessary steps to realizing your dream.

After reading this book and applying its ideas, you'll be committed to your dream and you'll be walking like a champion. *The Courage to Succeed* comes to life, because Ruben has written this book straight from his life experiences. An accomplished athlete and entrepreneur, Ruben pressed his way through the unfounded judgments of skeptics, broken bones, and zero sponsorship to become an Olympian...four times over. In four different decades! Ruben is candid and transparent about his difficulties and his successes in this book, and is just as candid and just as transparent about how his tenacious bulldog spirit transformed him into a winner.

There's a champion in all of us. Whether you're a struggling salesperson, an entrepreneur building a business, a student looking for better grades or a coach seeking to motivate your entire team to the state title, *The Courage to Succeed* will speak to you.

Read *The Courage to Succeed*. Read it carefully. Take it seriously. Follow through like Ruben. Do what Ruben says.

If you do what I say and carefully, seriously read this book and follow through with all of Ruben's good instruction, then you really will realize your goals and dreams.

Lou Holtz
Notre Dame Football Coach

A Word from the Author

My Dad always said to me, "If you read about the lives of people you admire, you'll learn what works and what doesn't work in life, because success leaves clues."

That was some of the best advice I've ever had. Over the years I've read hundreds of biographies, always looking for clues that would help me achieve my dreams and ambitions. Along the way I learned that successful people think differently. They have conditioned their minds to always focus on the possibilities, instead of the obstacles. Successful people think big, and then they make very wise choices. Because when it comes right down to it, success is a choice.

> *"All of our dreams can come true, if we have the courage to pursue them."*
> *– Walt Disney*

In order to consistently make the choices that lead to success, winners use two types of courage – the courage to act and the courage to endure – to never quit regardless of the circumstances. Understanding that they are bigger than their circumstances gives them the courage to succeed. You can learn to think and act like successful people do. Once you start thinking big, you'll start succeeding big, and that's what I want to help you do with this book.

As you read this book, I'll be hitting you with success principles from all different directions. Sometimes I'll repeat the timeless principles of success in order to help condition your subconscious mind to buy into these ideas and to begin acting on them.

If all you do is read this book, you'll be entertained with a great Olympic story. However, if you consistently and persistently apply the principles in this book, before long you'll be able to write your own success story.

When you read my story you'll realize that I'm just an ordinary person with an extraordinary dream. Once you see that, it will be that much easier for you to begin the pursuit of your dream.

Once you start winning battles on the way to your dream do me a favor - shoot me an email and share your victories with me. Your victories will fuel my victories.

Ruben Gonzalez
ruben@thelugeman.com
FourWinterGames.com

PART ONE

Against
All Odds

1988 Calgary Luge Ticket

1

"Life is either a daring adventure or nothing."

-Helen Keller

The Miracle in Lake Placid

They call it "The Miracle in Lake Placid." The date was February 22, 1980 – George Washington's Birthday. The story of David and Goliath was about to repeat itself.

The young, scrawny, inexperienced United States Hockey team was about to face the mighty Soviet Team at the Lake Placid Olympic Games. No one thought the Americans had a chance to win. They were just a hodgepodge squad made up of the top U.S. college players. The Americans had been playing together for only six months, so they had not even had a chance to "gel" - to get to know each other and become a real team.

The Soviet team was the best in the world. They were like a fine tuned machine. Some of the Soviet players had been playing together for 15 years. On any given play, they could confidently pass the puck to the open space, knowing that their teammate would be there to receive it. Six months earlier the Soviets had beaten the National Hockey League All Star team - arguably the strongest pro team in the U.S. Therefore, everyone expected the Soviets to steamroll the young American team.

Everyone, that is, except Herb Brooks, the U.S. Coach. Brooks believed in Team U.S.A. when no one else did. He told his players, "Realistically, we can beat the Russians about one out of ten times. We just have to make sure that this is the time. Our only chance is to attack the Russians, and play to win. Everyone else plays, not to lose. Our only chance is to attack, attack, attack!"

Brooks instilled his belief into his players. The young Americans attacked like they never had before. They played with confidence and boldness; with optimism and determination; they played to win. The young college kids trusted Brooks and kept shooting the puck; shot after shot after shot. The Soviets, not used to being attacked, were caught off guard. Somehow, the Americans pulled off one of the biggest upsets in Olympic history.

They beat the Russians 4-3. It really was a "Miracle in Lake Placid."

The crowd knew they had just experienced a once in a lifetime event, and they didn't want to leave the arena. After the game, the U.S. fans walked up and down Main Street Lake Placid. Almost on cue, snowflakes began to fall and for hours everyone walked and sang "The Star Spangled Banner," "America the Beautiful" and "God Bless America."

I was 17 years old when I witnessed the Miracle in Lake Placid. The hockey game reminded me of a dream I'd had ever since the third grade - a dream I'd buried because I didn't believe in myself. It was an improbable dream, an impossible dream, the dream of becoming an Olympian. At the end of the famous hockey game, when sports announcer Al Michaels exclaimed, "Do you believe in miracles?," I silently nodded my head and with fire in my eyes, said "Yes, I believe!"

Flash forward four years: it's 1984. Now I was walking down Main Street Lake Placid looking for the U.S. Olympic Training Center, where I was about to change my life forever by taking up the sport of luge with hopes of competing in the Calgary Winter Olympics four years later.

In 1984, I was a 21-year-old soccer player - a bench

warmer in my college team. Common logic would have dictated that I was much too old to start a new sport, but I was filled with a fire that had been rekindled by witnessing The Miracle four years earlier in Lake Placid.

This is the true story about how an ordinary person accomplished extraordinary things by simply believing. It's a story that takes the excuses away - a story that will inspire you to start believing in the possibility that you can make your dreams a reality too. Because, four years, and a few broken bones later, and against all odds, I was marching in the 1988 Calgary Winter Olympics, where I would be competing against the best in the world in the men's singles luge.

Acting in Spite of Your Fear

People always ask me, "What does it feel like to hurl down an icy chute at 90 miles per hour? Is it scary?"

Of course it's scary! I luged for 26 years, and until the last two years of my career, I still experienced fear during every run. The luge is like a water slide on steroids. It's been called "the last bit of insanity" left in the Olympics. The luge track is a mile-long chute of mean, slick, unforgiving, ice that starts 50 stories high. Fifty stories! That's way up!

It's like this. Imagine laying on a skateboard holding on to a 60 foot rope pulled behind a speeding Ferrari down a winding mountain road. Yeah. Down a mountain pass snaking left and right. Barely holding on. It's nuts! You're on the edge the whole way down. And if you fall off at 90 MPH? On the asphalt? What do you think? Is it going to hurt? Of course it hurts!

View from Men's Start, Igls, Austria.

The run down the mountain will take only about 50 seconds; albeit, the longest 50 seconds of your life. You'll be sliding down the track on a 50 pound, 4 foot long sled that's not much more than a piece of fiberglass on two steel runners. You know you'll be reaching neck-breaking speeds of almost 90 miles per hour, and you'll be getting squashed as you pull up to 6 G's around the curves, and you have no brakes! Does this seem normal so far?

I have to admit, though, that the luge is a terrible sport for television because on TV, it doesn't look like we are doing anything. People who watch us on TV think all we do is hold on and pray. Well, they're two-thirds right. We hold on and pray, but we also steer a lot. We're making hundreds of tiny corrections to have the best line down the track, the best trajectory that will get us to the finish line in the least amount of time.

When you're driving your car on a freeway, small movements on the steering wheel make a big difference. The luge is no different. Tiny movements make a huge difference in the luge. All you have to do is press down with your shoulder, and the sled steers right or left. If you turn your head a couple of inches to the left or right, the sled responds. Making a movement as small as a hiccough could cause you to slam into a wall. Once that happens, you're in trouble, because you start "ping-ponging" back and forth, hitting the left and right wall, and there's not much you can do to stop it. When your feet keep slamming onto the rock-hard iced walls, it's very easy to fracture bones. If it's your turn to go and you get the hiccoughs, you better brace yourself. Because you're going to have a wild ride!

Even your breathing makes a difference in the luge. We are taught to exhale when we approach the entrance and exit of every curve. Exhaling helps you relax. The more relaxed and loose you are, the faster your reaction time and the faster you go. The top lugers in the circuit have been sliding since they were ten years old. Ten-year-olds are bulletproof. They don't fear anything. By the time they are old enough to know better, they have developed solid fundamentals; consequently, they are able to remain totally relaxed down the whole run. They have no problem breathing calmly the whole way down.

When you see the top guys luging, they look as relaxed as someone lying on a hammock reading a paperback. With me, though, it's different. I got started so late that I've never gotten past the fear. After about a third of the way down, the fear from the high speeds causes me to forget to breathe and I become a "white-knuckled slider." When I'm luging, I don't look like a guy relaxing on a hammock. I look like a cowboy riding a wild bull!

Like I said, though, watching the luge on TV is about as exciting as watching grass grow. But live and in person, the luge is unbelievable. It surprisingly becomes a real spectator sport. You're standing just a couple of feet away from a

20 foot wall of ice, and suddenly, you hear eerie sounds, rumbling, thundering sounds as sleds smash and pummel against ice, and the crashing gets louder and louder as they near. Suddenly, a blur shoots across the ice with a whoosh and disappears down the track. As they shoot by, you are close enough to them, that you can actually feel the wind from their sled as it whizzes on by.

If it's snowing and snow is accumulating on the track, as the sleds race by, they seem to leave a puff of white smoke behind them, a wake of snow, like when a car speeds over a road covered with fallen leaves. One instant you see the sled, and then all you see is the snow rolling down the track. It's almost surreal and unnatural, as if you'd just seen a ghost fly by.

Both above and below you, athletes are bearing down the run, no more than a flash to your eye. They wear a helmet and a racing suit so tight that they look like they've been held by the nose and dipped in high-gloss paint.

This uniform actually makes them look like human rockets painting streaks in the ice as they flash by. You are so close to the action that you can lean over, look a luger in the eye, and feel the rush of wind they stir up as they bolt down the run. For an instant, their blazing images become frozen in your mind.

Studying each racer and coaching their every move with your eyes, you are swept up in their momentum. At times, you might ask yourself, "Will he make it? Is this really a race? Maybe they aren't racing. Maybe they are being sacrificed." As soon as the luger rockets by, your eyes are drawn back up the mountain – where you can't help but be excited as you look for the next victim.

Fortune Favors the Brave

What's it actually feel like to take a luge run? Fasten your seatbelt.

Walking up to the start, you can look down the mountain and see the entire length of the track. The hair stands up on the back of your neck. Your stomach gets queasy. Your mouth gets dry. Why? Because you know what can happen down there – broken bones, dislocations, concussions... and worse. Over the years I've broken my foot twice, my knee, my elbow, my hand, my thumb, and a few ribs. My neck is a chiropractor's dream. They find things there that they've never seen before.

Sitting on the sled, you know that in a few seconds, you'll be launching into the most exhilarating athletic event of your life. Closing your eyes, you take a mental run, imagining exactly how you'll steer each curve. Opening your eyes, you take three deep breaths and fasten the visor on the helmet. Gripping the start handles, you rock once...twice... and then pull with everything you've got. You're off...

Digging into the ice, paddling furiously like a kayaker upstream, your muscles pull and strain to employ the spiked luge gloves. Luge gloves deliver the traction a luger requires for a powerful, speedy launch from the starting gate. Then you lay down on the sled and try to assume the shape of a human bullet as you race down the icy tube...

Shooting down the track, the speed and fear increase dramatically. In no time, you are blazing at speeds up to seventy, eighty, ninety miles per hour. At these speeds, the world seems to turn into a blur. You feel as if you're riding a bar of soap. Everything happens so fast.

You focus your eyes about 30 feet in front of you and everything else becomes tunnel vision. You are so focused that you don't even hear the spectators screaming. Yes, screaming. When a luge comes barreling down the track, there is so much adrenaline in the air that the spectators can't help but whoop and holler. The scream follows the sled all the way down the track. But you don't hear them. The spectators could be shooting guns up into the air like a bunch of crazy Texans and you would not hear them. You don't hear them because every cell in your body is intently focused on driving the right line. It's that intense. I've never experienced anything as intense as the luge. Nothing comes even close. Nothing.

Sometimes you ride 20 feet high on the curved walls. You pull as many as six G's. That's more than twice the G's astronauts experience on takeoff. I weigh 200 lbs. Six G's feels like you have 1200 lbs. squashing you. It feels like a polar bear is sitting on your chest.

Zipping by trees and crowds you somehow try to stay relaxed. You bump a wall, your teeth chatter and your vision gets blurry.

All the way down the track, you are right on the ragged edge of control - right on the edge of disaster. Remember when you were a kid, and you leaned back on a chair balancing on its back legs and felt the point where balance is lost and you were about to fall back? That's exactly what the luge feels like. Like an out of balance chair moving 90 miles per hour.

You are managing risk the entire way down the luge run. Do you dare to take a faster, more risky line down the track? You can actually "cut-corners" down the luge track, but doing so increases the chance of slamming into a wall and crashing. Do you dare put your head back for a few seconds and race blindly to be more aerodynamic? Tucking your head back to assume the shape of a bullet will make the sled go faster, but when you do, you won't see where you are going. Do you dare round your steel runners to give up traction and gain speed?

That's what the top guys in the luge circuit do. They

actually ride on sleds that have virtually no traction, and they race blindly (using only their peripheral vision) the whole way down. That's what it takes to win Olympic Gold. It's risky business to dare to become a world class luger.

Successful people don't avoid risk. They embrace and manage risk to have the opportunity to win more. On the circuit, the top competitors are the ones who are so mentally tough that they are willing to take the biggest risks. To win big you have to be willing to risk big. When somebody crashes on the luge, nobody laughs. They respect you for pushing the envelope. They respect you for going for it.

At the end of the luge run you are exhausted, out of breath and soaked in sweat even though the temperature might be twenty below outside. Your muscles are tight, you have a pounding headache, and you feel completely worn out. Drained. The combination of the cold, the G-force pressure against the curves, the stress, and the fear is so hard on the body, that four or five training runs a day is all we can endure. Usually two runs in the morning and three in the afternoon. One time, in Lake Placid, we took ten runs in one day, and we ended up missing the next day's training because our joints hurt just like when you have the flu.

If you want to win big, you have to be willing to lose big.

As you cross the finish line, you sit up on the sled to start slowing down, and "BOOM!" you get slammed with a 90 mile per hour blast of air right on your chest. Literally, from an open free form speed of ninety miles per hour, you force yourself to sit up on the sled to bring your speed down to… zero. It takes about 200 yards to come to a stop. The length of two football fields!

As soon as you step off the sled the adrenaline rush hits you. The fear hits you like a sledgehammer. Wheeeeeww!!!!

End of run, Lake Placid, NY.

The fear makes you say, "I'm never doing that again! Why am I putting myself through this? I must be nuts. I quit!"

And all of a sudden you realize how cold you are. After all, it's below zero outside, you've been experiencing a ridiculous wind-chill factor, and all you're wearing is a t-shirt and a spandex suit. The wild ride you just took left you drenched in sweat, and you start shivering.

You say to yourself, "Why did I even pick the luge? I must have been nuts! That's it. I'm going back to soccer. Soccer's warm, it's soft, and it's fun. Forget luge." You want to quit with every fiber of your being. You really do. Walking around in disgust for a few seconds, you shake your head and try to calm down. "I need some help. I have to get some help…"

Thank Goodness, there is a tool, a saving grace to help you. There's a walkie-talkie waiting for you at the finish with familiar voices ready to help. Up and down the whole track, there are coaches watching each luger, waiting to give words of encouragement and instruction. The coaches can see things you can't. They actually videotape lugers in their practice runs and, later that night, take time to review the tapes with you to see what improvements must be made to be faster the next day. No matter how well you did today, you can do even better tomorrow. There is always a higher level you can aspire to.

My coach is Günther Lemmerer, a four-time Olympian and a three-time World Champion from Austria. Günther is about 6'6". He looks and sounds like Arnold Schwarzenegger. Coach is tough as nails. He could have been a Marine drill sergeant. When Coach says, "Jump," I say, "How high?"

Coach isn't just an expert. He was the best – a legend in the sport. He didn't just read about it. He did it. He won three World Championships in doubles luge – each time with a different teammate. No one else in the sport has ever accomplished that. Most doubles teams team up for life. They get to know each other's style and nuances so they think in unison as they are racing down the track. Imagine winning the pairs figure skating Championship, changing partners, winning it a second time, changing partners again, and going on to win the Championship for a third time. That's what Coach did. Coach was the common denominator in winning those three championships; he made the difference. Coach has the fruit on the trees. Learning the luge from Coach is like learning basketball from Michael Jordan. I trust Coach and I do whatever he says.

As I'm still gasping for breath from my wild run, I pick up the walkie-talkie, and say, "Coach, this is Ruben."

Coach says, "Ruben, Nach Cmmon!" Nach Cmmon

Coach and I in Königsee, Germany

roughly means "No Ruben, come on! What's wrong with you?" And the way Coach says it makes it clear that he is really upset, disenchanted, and disillusioned with my performance. Whenever Coach says "Nach Cmmon," I know the next thing out of his mouth won't be good. My knees are starting to shake...

"Ruben, you must point your toes more, and put your head further back! And Ruben you were so late into curve 6. You must steer harder, harder, harder on curve 6. And Ruben, you must relax, relax, be one with the sled..."

Yeah, right! You try relaxing when you're going 90 miles per hour! Sometimes, I finish the luge run and think I was relaxed. As soon as I pick up the walkie-talkie, Coach says, "Ruben, you must relax!" Arrgh!

You think *your* boss is tough? In fifteen years, the best comment I ever got out of Coach after a run was, "Ruben, that was not so bad."

14

Even when Coach says a run was not so bad, he says it in an exasperated, annoyed manner. I can picture him rolling his eyes as he's saying it. I know he must be thinking "I can't believe what Ruben is doing out there!" But it doesn't matter. When Coach tells you, "That was not so bad," you want to celebrate.

Never Ever Quit

In the last twenty six years I've taken thousands of luge runs. I've wanted to quit after every single one. Why? Because for me it is so, so... intense. So... extreme. So... terrifying at times. Having gotten started so late in the sport, the luge has never felt natural to me. I've never developed a feel for it. It has never felt like a recreational sport to me; I'm too much on the edge to enjoy it. I'd much rather be playing soccer, basketball, squash or ping pong.

But after talking to Coach, I'm thinking, "I know exactly what I'm going to do next run. I'm pointing my toes, my head's going back, I'm steering harder, harder, harder on curve 6, I'm going to relax, and lookout, I'll be faster than ever before!"

It only takes talking to Coach for 30 seconds to get me back on the sled. In those thirty seconds, Coach takes my focus off of my obstacles and puts my focus back on to my objective – the Olympics. After all, the luge is just the vehicle: the Olympics is the dream. Many times the road to your dreams is a rough one. When it is, you need all the help and encouragement you can get. If it had not been for Coach, I never would have made it to the Olympics.

I've got news for you. You will have bad days. You will have bad weeks. You will have bad months. Once in a while you'll even have a bad year. I have. I've had years when it seemed that no matter how hard I worked, nothing worked out; times when I questioned and doubted myself; times when I was so discouraged all I wanted to do was quit.

Thank God that I latched on to my Coach's belief in me when I didn't believe in myself. Thank God that I listened when Coach explained to me that even though I was not getting the results I wanted, I was gaining experience and was growing into the type of person that would get those results down the road. Thank God that I listened to Coach. Because he was a constant source of power and strength.

Winners focus on the goal, not on the obstacles.

How about you? What do you do when the going gets tough? When life hits you with storms? Do you try to figure it out for yourself? Do you start feeling sorry for yourself and go out and have a pity party?

Do you start blaming circumstances instead of taking responsibility? Do you get frustrated, then discouraged to the point where you quit? The next time you're in the middle of one of life's storms, you're discouraged, and you're starting to doubt yourself, don't go out and try to figure it out on your own. The worst time to make a decision is when things are not going your way.

If you do that, you'll be basing your decision entirely on emotion - not on intellect. If you make a decision when you're down, you're bound to make a bad decision. That's when you're the closest to quitting.

When things are not going your way, pick up the walkie-talkie. Pick up the phone. Talk to your husband, your wife, your best friend, your coach, your mentor or your boss. Talk to someone who cares for you; someone who believes in you; someone who will get you back on the sled; someone who will get you back on track; someone who won't let you quit, because if you quit on your dream, you'll regret it all your life. Guaranteed.

16

Hope Accomplishes the Impossible

I share my story to give you hope; to help you see that you were designed for greatness; to make you understand that you must believe in yourself.

You see, if you believe something is possible, and have hope, then you will not quit. Hope sees the invisible. Hope accomplishes the impossible. Napoleon said that a leader's most important job is to give hope to his troops – to show them that success is possible; Coach constantly reminds me that there is hope. If you have hope you will take action. And once you take action you're on the path to success. As soon as you lose hope you quit.

People ask me how I keep my hope up. They ask me why I'm willing to train so hard for so long for the Olympics – especially knowing that the probability of medaling is so, so slim. When asked that, I feel just like mountain climbers must feel when they are asked, "Why do you climb mountains?" When someone asks you that, you don't even want to bother answering, because they just don't understand. They don't get it. And so you end up saying something profound like, "Because it's there."

Why do it? To fulfill an urge, a powerful inner calling to take a journey that will show us what we are made of. Climbing the mountain or making the attempt for the Olympics is a challenge that allows us test ourselves so we can know ourselves better.

Why work so hard? Because doing the work buys us an opportunity, a chance, however small, to medal. Doing the roadwork, the pushups, the sit-ups and the insanely boring weightlifting, makes us stronger both physically and mentally. The hours and hours of sled work before every race (we spend hours polishing our steel runners before

17

every race to remove even microscopic nicks that could slow us down the mountain), make us stronger mentally as well. With every stroke of fine sandpaper on the steels, we are making the sled faster. With every stroke we know our chances to medal are better. Why work so hard? Because there is a possibility that I will medal. It's not probable, but it's possible. Because in life, as long as you don't quit you still have a chance, you still have hope.

Stop making excuses and start believing in yourself,

> *When there's hope in the future, there's power in the present.*

because you are bigger than your circumstances and because you were created to accomplish great things. You were. When you read my story, you will see that if you want something badly enough and you're willing to go for it, dreams do come true.

Whether you want to be a better mom or dad, a better wife or husband, a better employee, a better boss, a better salesperson... whether your dream is to travel the world, or move to a beautiful home in the mountains or by the beach, no matter what your dream is, all it takes to succeed is guts and vision; the vision to know what you want, and the guts to go for it and to never quit.

My story takes the excuses away because although I was not a great athlete, my Olympic dream still became a reality four times. The only reason my dream was realized is because I consistently and persistently followed some universal success principles. Principles I learned while growing up; while training for the Olympics; and from the Olympic Games themselves. Principles you can follow to win too.

Now, through my story, I'll share these principles with you.

You Will Only See It
When You Believe It

I was born in Argentina. My dad was a chemical engineer with Exxon. We moved to the United States in 1968 when I was 6 years old.

We lived in Queens, New York. I didn't speak a word of English. To make matters worse, I was the only kid in my class who didn't speak English.

School-kids are constantly trying to determine what the pecking order will be; and so they pick on each other. I know you were picked on in school, because everyone gets picked on sometime or another. Remember how you felt when somebody picked on you? Didn't it make you feel insignificant? Like you were worthless?

Even adults pick on each other. Some people never outgrow it. There's probably someone in your workplace that is always giving everyone else a hard time. The ironic thing is that the "bullies" feel insignificant as well. The problem is bullies think that the only way for them to look good is by pushing everybody else down.

In school, kids look for anything that makes you different and they use that as a justification for picking on you. Not speaking English, and consequently, not speaking to anyone, made me an easy target for the school bullies. It was terrible. One day, while in the first grade, I was actually stabbed, with a pencil – by a girl!

I got picked everywhere but the one place where I wanted to get picked: P.E. When kids were picking teams to play sports I never was chosen. You see, I didn't know how to play any of the American games, like football, baseball, or dodge ball. My dad didn't know how to play them either, so he couldn't help me.

In Argentina, kids played soccer. Soccer is the only sport

anyone cares about in Argentina. However, soccer wasn't very popular in the U.S. in 1968. Consequently, I was never chosen to play sports in P.E.

After enduring the rejections for awhile, I thought there had to be something wrong with me. Any day of the week, I could have told you what color the shoes on my feet were because I walked around all day looking at them.

Allowing those bullies' opinion of me to become my reality was a big mistake. After all, those kids were just being kids. I should not have taken it personally. They didn't know me or understand me. Eleanor Roosevelt said, "No one can make you feel inferior without your consent." I gave them my consent and you may be doing the same thing. Perhaps, someone who does not know or understand you said something to you and you bought into it. Maybe someone made fun of you or called you stupid, or dumb, or slow. Perhaps they said you were not cut out to do what your heart tells you to do with your life. Now that belief is holding you back from what you are capable of doing. Don't listen to them. You're bigger than you realize. Don't let someone else's opinion of you become your reality.

> **Don't let other people's opinion of you become your reality.**

Small people cut achievers down because they believe that's the only way for them to look good. Insecure people feel threatened anytime others try to do something great with their lives. Consequently, they will do anything they can to make you feel inferior. You need to feel good when people start making fun of you, because when they do, it shows you are starting to go places. If nobody is criticizing you, you're probably not doing much.

Of course, I didn't know all of that then. I just thought there was something wrong with me. And so, as a kid, filled with rejection, I withdrew from others and became a loner. I spent most of my free time doing two things: kicking a soccer ball and reading. I kicked a soccer ball against a wall for hours dreaming of someday being a professional soccer player. That's every Argentinean boy's dream.

My other favorite activity was reading books about people who lived adventurous lives; books like "Around the World in 80 Days" and "20,000 Leagues under the Sea." I learned how to speak English by reading adventure books.

By the time I could speak English, I would tell the other kids, "I want my life to be like a book."

They would ask me, "What do you mean?"

My reply would be, "I want my life to be filled with adventures!"

People tend to get what they think about, focus on, and act on. By having my "antennas" out looking for adventures, I found mine. One day, at the age of ten, while still in the third grade, as I was watching the Olympics on TV for the first time in my life, the Olympic dream got a hold of me. That day I knew that becoming an Olympian would be my adventure.

What I admired most about the Olympians was not necessarily their athleticism, but rather their spirit. You see, right away I realized that this was a group of people that were willing to put everything on the line to realize their dreams. They were willing to go for it with no guarantees of success. They were willing to train for years and years and then, some of them finally made it. Filled with wonder, I thought to myself, "Wow, you have to be so mentally strong and courageous to go for it all."

The Olympians were everything that I wasn't. Therefore, I placed all of them high up on a pedestal, and my deep admiration for them made me yearn become an Olympian.

From that day on, I became an Olympic expert. Reading everything I could get my hands on about the Olympics, in no time I could tell you the stats on every athlete, everything about Olympic history and all about Olympic philosophy. However, fear of failure and lack of belief in myself kept me from taking action. I wasn't an Olympic expert. I was just an "Olympic groupie."

How to Raise Your Self-Belief Level

What the mind conceives and believes, it can achieve. I had conceived the Olympic Dream, but I still did not believe in myself. I needed to start believing in myself in order to get myself to take action. By not believing in myself, I was just operating out of wishful thinking. I was hoping the Olympics would drop on my lap. Lack of self-belief or lack of confidence, results in fear of failure, and that's what keeps people from pursuing their dreams. After all, if you don't believe you can achieve your dream, why even try? Once you believe, you are ready to commit to taking action. And believe me, success requires taking MASSIVE ACTION – for a long time. Unless you commit, you'll never make your dream come true.

Most people need to believe more in themselves but they don't know how. For a long time I didn't know how. Fortunately there are a couple of things you can do to raise your belief level. The books you read and the people you associate with will ultimately determine what you believe.

After a couple of years, my dad grew tired of listening to me "talk the talk" but not "walk the walk." Dad knew three things about me; that I needed a boost of confidence, that I liked to read, and that I was so hard-headed that I would probably not listen to anything he told me until I was 30 years old.

Taking all of this into account, my dad did something very smart. Rather than give me the information directly, and risk having me reject it, he gave me the information indirectly; he led me to the source of the information. That way, Dad knew I would think I had discovered it on my own.

"Ruben," my dad began, "you like to read. Why don't you read some biographies – the stories of great people. If you read about the lives of people you look up to, people you admire, you'll learn what works and what doesn't work in life, because success leaves clues." Then he backed off. And let the books work their magic.

I thought, "Biographies sound just like adventure stories, only these are true-life adventures." I started reading biographies and started loving them. I read tons of them. My favorites were the stories of people who had overcome great odds to realize their dreams, people like; Wilma Rudolph,

Mom holding my brother Marcelo and Dad holding me.

> *The lives of successful people are filled with clues we can use to succeed in our own lives.*

who overcame polio to become an Olympic Champion in track at the 1960 Rome Summer Olympics, General Patton, who moved his armies faster than anyone thought possible, and Louis Pasteur, who's belief in bacteria's role in causing disease led him to invent pasteurization and to discover a cure for rabies.

Dream. Struggle. Victory.

Before long, I realized that every biography is the same story. It's the story of someone who had a dream, went through a struggle, and finally experienced a victory. It's always dream, struggle, victory. Dream, struggle, victory, and then, someone shows up and wants to write a book about you.

One of the many things that biographies taught me was that these people were not born great. At one point, these extraordinary people were ordinary people just like me. It was the struggle that made them great. The struggle forced them to dig down deep inside themselves. And only when they dug deep inside themselves did they find their gifts.

That knowledge gave me hope. The hope that if I followed in their footsteps, maybe I could accomplish great things too. It made me realize that success is not about luck, success is a process.

I set out to find one single quality that all these people I was reading about had in common. A quality that I could focus on one hundred percent. The quality they all had in common was perseverance. Perseverance gave them

24

the staying power to not quit when the going got tough. Perseverance allowed them to stay in the game long enough to learn the skills they would need to succeed.

Every one of these people went through a stage in their lives when they were doing nothing but hitting their heads on the wall. Many times these people spent twenty years in the struggle; years and years trying to figure out a way to make their dreams a reality. And along the way there were always people who rejected them or laughed at them. But they believed so much in their mission, that they refused to quit.

Don't take my word for it. Read about people like the Wright Brothers, who worked for years before their airplane finally flew. Look at Henry Ford, who built a single block engine when even all his engineers said it couldn't be done. Look at Abraham Lincoln, who overcame depression, bankruptcy, and seemingly endless political defeats before he won his first election.

Their perseverance always paid off in the long run. By refusing to quit, one of two things always happened: they either figured out a way to make their dream a reality through sheer trial-and-error, or else they met someone who showed them the ropes; someone who helped them out; someone who became their mentor.

However, neither of these things had a chance of occurring unless they had first made a decision to hang on and persevere no matter what.

Great people have two types of courage. They have the courage to get started; to take a leap of faith; to take action when they have no guarantees of success. Once they are on their way, they develop the courage to endure. The courage to not quit. The courage to persevere. Perseverance is the key.

That knowledge helped me make a quality decision that completely changed my life...

The Key to Success

One day, after having read many biographies, while still in the fifth grade, I decided that from that day on, I would not quit anything. I realized that if I quit when the going got tough, then the next time the going got tough it would be easy to quit again. If I kept doing that, quitting would just become a bad habit.

If all you ever do is quit everything you begin, twenty years go by and then you realize that you have not accomplished anything with your life. I didn't want that to happen to me.

Aristotle said that we become what we repeatedly do. Every time you face your fears, you become more courageous. Every time you refuse to quit, you become more perseverant. The more you persist in the face of adversity, the more you like and respect yourself.

I simply decided to quit quitting. And that's a decision you can make this instant. Will you? It's a decision that will change your life. If a hard-headed fifth grader can make that decision you surely can. Will you?

A few years went by. One day, as a sophomore in high school, this kid came up to me and said, "Ruben, your nickname should be Bulldog."

I said, "Why?"

"Because bulldogs never quit. If a bulldog gets a hold of your leg, he's not letting go," the kid said.

"Is that right?" I said. I didn't know that about bulldogs.

"Sure it's right."

I went to the library to check on this newly discovered fact about bulldogs. Being a pretty skeptical person, I always check the truth about matters. He was right. Bulldogs are known for tenacity. Bulldogs were actually bred to be tenacious; they were bred to fight bulls to the death in arenas like the ancient Coliseum. Their lower jaw is longer than their upper jaw so that when they bit a bull, they did not have

26

to ever let go to breathe. I loved the idea of being tenacious like a bulldog!

From that day on, whenever I met somebody, I'd say, "Hi, my name is Ruben, but you can call me Bulldog!"

By doing that I was putting positive pressure on myself to not ever quit. Imagine how embarrassing it would be to be known as "Bulldog" and be a quitter. A little positive pressure goes a long way.

The other thing that reading biographies did for me was to give me hope. Invariably, when picking up a biography from a bookshelf, I'd look at the person on the cover and think to myself, "I could never be like them." Immediately, the person on the cover would go up on a pedestal.

Invariably, as I read the biography, I'd be reminded that when the person on the cover was young, they had been an ordinary person just like I was. It was the struggle that had made them great.

Reading biographies gave me hope; hope that I could accomplish great things, just as these people had accomplished provided I was willing to put myself through a struggle to reach my goals. Reading biographies gave me hope and taught me that I needed perseverance to succeed.

By the way, if you don't like to read, no problem. Just tune in to the Biography Channel and you'll learn the same things that I learned. You'll learn it from people like Ray Kroc, a paper cup salesman, who developed the McDonald's Restaurant System when he was in his fifties, or, Harland Sanders, who didn't start Kentucky Fried Chicken until after he was retired, or, Lewis and Clark, who literally went into the unknown to find routes to the west. The list goes on and on. You'll see that age and circumstances really don't matter as long as you want something badly enough and are willing to do the work.

Teaming Up with Winners to Win Big

The other thing my Dad always told me was to watch out who I associated with. He always encouraged me to surround myself with winners. Dad would say, "You need to hang around people you have respect for, not people you have influence over."

"If all you ever do is hang around people you have influence over, you're like the big fish in the small pond. Sure it feels good – you're the big shot. But since no one is pushing you, since no one is challenging you, you never get any better.

Dad said I needed to force myself to hang around successful people. Successful people think big. They are always focusing on the possibilities. They are always asking themselves, "What if?," "Why not?," "Why wait?"

My dad said I would feel uncomfortable, out of place, and like I didn't belong. But, if I hung around big thinkers long enough, eventually, I would begin to think big, too. Dad said that successful people would always challenge me and encourage me to be my best; to continuously strive to reach higher levels of performance. They would always be a "phone call away" or like Coach, "a walkie-talkie away" to steer me right.

My father added that when those successful people started to believe in me, I would begin to believe in myself, too, because I respected their opinions. And that's exactly what happened.

Sometimes, to develop a belief system in yourself, you have to trust the opinions and beliefs others have in you until you gain confidence and your own belief system kicks in.

Over a period of time, by reading great books and associating with winners I began to believe more and more in myself. I started buying into what they were telling me - that everyone has the seeds of greatness within themselves.

For several years I played soccer in small neighborhood teams. Since my high school didn't have a soccer team, I thought that playing college soccer was out of the question. When you think about it, that does not even make sense. It's so easy for self-limiting beliefs to hold us back.

Fortunately, through reading good books and listening to successful people, I began to take more risks. I started exploring the outside of the envelope. Little by little I started realizing that the sky is the limit. Taking chances and facing my fears made me believe more and more in myself.

Many times we allow self-limiting beliefs to hold us back. What's holding you back? What's keeping you from burning all the bridges and pursuing your dream? Lack of money? Lack of time? Lack of information? Fear of failure?

Surround yourself with winners.

Ninety percent of success comes from who you regularly associate with.

Winners will always lift you up. Losers will always pull you down.

Who are you associating with?

Don't Listen to Your Fears

I finally came to the realization that there was nothing to lose by trying out for the local college soccer team. I tried out, made the team and even got a scholarship!

What if I had listened to my self-limiting beliefs? I would have missed out on the wonderful experience of playing college sports. Don't listen your fears. Do what you fear and the fear will disappear.

All of a sudden, I was playing soccer for Houston Baptist University. NCAA Division I Soccer, but just as a second stringer. Despite the fact that I had played soccer for years, I wasn't fast, I couldn't jump high, and, overall, I was just an average athlete.

> *Don't take council of your fears. Do what you fear and the fear will disappear.*

But it didn't matter. I was on the team. I was finally on the team! Being on a real team for the first time in my life, my ego could not handle the possibility of getting cut from that team. As a result, I was willing to do whatever it took to stay on the team.

The other players on the team were so talented, that I knew that no matter how hard I worked, I probably would not get to play much. It didn't matter. I just wanted to be on the team. I decided to let my work ethic become an example to the team. That would be my contribution. I worked harder than I ever had in my life. And Coach just kept me on the team because I inspired the other players to practice harder.

Coach laid down the rule. He said, "Ruben doesn't play unless we're up by two goals." Two Goals! That kind of scoring hardly ever happens in soccer. I guess I was a threat to my own team. As long as I was not on the field, we had a chance. I only played about five minutes a game, but it didn't

Warming my soccer team's bench.

matter. I was part of the team.

Something special happened during my last season. Whenever we were up by one goal, it seemed like the whole team would start playing harder. Maybe they wanted to score that second goal so I could play a few minutes. I don't know. What I do know is that on my last season, whenever we were up by one goal we never lost a game. That year our team had the best won-lost record in the U.S. - 18 wins and only 2 losses. Team HBU ranked as high as 20th in the nation – out of hundreds of teams.

I have to believe that our soccer team would not have done as well if I had not been part of it. As long as I wasn't on the field, we had a chance. But I made those guys play harder. What I learned from that is that no matter what part of the team you are, if you do your best you do make a difference.

Top twenty in the nation and Conference Champs

Everyone is important. Every role is important. Even the water boy is important. If the water boy does not show up, the team loses the game in the second half. They do, because the players need water to be able to play hard all game long.

Martin Luther King said, "If you are called to be a street sweeper, sweep streets even as Michelangelo painted, or Beethoven composed music, or Shakespeare wrote poetry. Sweep streets so well that all the hosts of heaven and earth will pause to say, 'Here lived a great street sweeper who did his job well.'"

Take pride in whatever you're doing. Don't ever get that "stinking thinking" that nobody appreciates you or that you can't make a difference. Everyone can make a difference. Everyone.

Take Charge of Your Life

At twenty-one, I was finally a "big jock" (a legend in my own mind) and my self belief was higher than ever. Napoleon Hill, the author of "Think and Grow Rich," said "What the mind can conceive and believe it can achieve." For the first time in my life I believed in myself.

The Olympics rolled around again. I was glued to the TV watching the 1984 Sarajevo Winter Olympic Games when I saw something that changed my life.

I saw a little guy, all of about five feet tall who couldn't have weighed more than a hundred ten pounds soaking wet. This tough, 18-year-old was set on winning the Olympic Gold Medal in figure skating. His name: Scott Hamilton.

When I saw Scott Hamilton win his medal and when I learned about his story, he gave me hope. After all, Scott Hamilton had overcome so much. From age five to eight, he had suffered from a disease that kept him from digesting food and from growing. I said to myself, "If that little guy can do it, I can do it too! I'm going to be in the next Olympics! It's a done deal. I just have to find a sport." I sure wasn't going to make it to the Olympics playing soccer!

I'd been playing soccer since I was a little kid. Tens of thousands of hours of practice, and even with this much time and effort, I was barely good enough to sit on the bench. And I'm going to take up a new sport at the age of twenty-one and compete in the Olympics in four years? Is that realistic?

If you want something badly enough, if you believe you can do it, and you are willing to do whatever it takes, for however long it takes, then anything is realistic.

If you are willing to do whatever it takes for as long as it takes, success is just a matter of time.

When the why is big enough, the how will take care of itself.

Base Your Plan on
Your Strengths

When the "why" is big enough, the "how" will take care of itself. Armed with a powerful reason and belief in myself, I was ready to find a way. I was ready to start taking action.

I went to the library to take a look at the list of Olympic sports. After looking at the list of summer sports, such as; the discus, the high jump, and the marathon, I realized that, "You have to be some kind of a super-athlete to do any of these things – there's no way!" After all, most summer sports require sudden bursts of speed and power – neither of which I had.

As I was looking at the Winter Olympic sports, it occurred to me that, "I'm about to put together a plan for the next four years. It might make sense to base the plan on my strengths."

My strength wasn't athletic ability. My strength was perseverance, tenacity, stick-to-iveness. I wasn't a quitter. I was Bulldog.

Therefore, the challenge was to find a sport so tough, a sport so dangerous, a sport that resulted in so many broken bones, that there would be a lot of quitters. Let everyone else quit. That way, maybe I could rise to the top through the attrition rate.

Now I was looking for tough sports, sports that required skill and tenacity, sports such as; ski jump, bobsled, luge.

I lived in hot and humid Houston, Texas, not exactly the winter sports capital of the United States. I'd never even skied before, so forget the ski jump – that would have been suicide. And finding three other nuts in Houston that wanted to do the bobsled was going to be very unlikely. Forget bobsled. But luge, I could do by myself. I'd never even seen the luge on TV. If I had, maybe I wouldn't have done the luge either.

Ask for Help to Win More

When I decided to take up the luge and train for the Olympics, I was a cocky 21-year-old kid. I thought I could do it by myself. Obviously, I still had a lot of growing up to do.

In "Seven Habits of Highly Effective People," Stephen Covey talks about three stages people go through – dependence, independence, and interdependence. When you are in the dependent stage, you depend on others for everything, like a child. Then as you move into the independent stage, you are like a teenager – you think you can do everything by yourself. Finally, in the interdependent stage, you learn that much more can be achieved by creating and working through teams of people. At twenty-one, I was still in the independent stage. I needed to learn to ask for help from other people. I needed to become more interdependent in order to build a team that would make it easier to achieve my dream.

It didn't take long for me to realize that I was going to need some help. In order to accomplish great things, I was going to have to develop some leadership and people skills to build a team. Then, I would have to work through the team to make my Olympic dream come true. I was going to have to turn singles luge into a team sport, finding people who could help me, coach me, and encourage me.

This mentality is a philosophy and it is no different from launching any big project or endeavor. "Lone Rangers" never accomplish as much as the type of people who work in and through teams.

The Secret to Becoming a Winner

Everything rises and falls on leadership. It always has and it always will, because by working through other people, a good leader can accomplish infinitely more than a single person. Leadership is becoming a person of influence. It's attracting followers. If you're the leader, you look back and nobody is following you, guess what? You're not the leader.

If you want to be the leader in your family, in your business, in your community or in your church, you need two things: passion and integrity. If you are passionate about your mission, you will attract the people who are like minded; people who would like to be a part of your mission.

I passionately told everyone about my Olympic dream. Everyone. I was not wishy-washy, I was excited. Other people had no doubt that I believed in and was committed to my dream, because they could see it in my eyes.

By being passionate and enthusiastic about my dream, whenever I talked to someone who had an interest in the Olympics, I became their link to the Olympic Games. And many times they were willing to help me. Believe me, I needed a lot of help.

I needed financial help. It's very expensive to fly all over the world to train and compete. You're also out of work for months at a time. Everyone thinks I have corporate sponsors. People always ask me, "Ruben, who are your sponsors? Coke? Pepsi? Nike?" I laugh and say, "My sponsors are Visa and MasterCard baby! I put it all on my credit card." After my credit cards reached their limit, my family lent me tens of thousands of dollars. That's just part of the price of success.

I also needed medical help from Doctors, chiropractors, and physical therapists in order to stay healthy and to patch up the scrapes, bruises, and broken bones after bad crashes. You don't even have to crash to get hurt in the luge. If you enter a curve incorrectly, you get hammered with much higher G forces at the apex of the curve. Since your head hangs at the end of the sled, your neck takes a beating.

Have you ever had a stiff neck? When you have a stiff neck, any movement makes it feel like somebody is stabbing you. You just want to lie down and rest. During the Salt Lake City Olympics, my neck was strained so badly, that I had to get a chiropractic adjustment and a neck massage between every run. Imagine sitting at the start of a luge run with a stiff neck knowing that as soon as you hit the ice, your head is going to be shaken up like a maraca in a Latin band.

Finally, I needed people who would keep my spirits up when I was struggling; people who would keep me from quitting. The first couple of years in the luge are brutal. I was crashing four out of five times. Most luge tracks have fifteen curves. When you are learning the sport of luge, the coach might start you off from curve ten; two thirds of the way down. You're only reaching speeds of about thirty miles per hour. After a few runs from curve ten, the coach moves you up a couple of curves. Now you are sliding at forty miles per hour. All of a sudden, since your mind is used to reacting at thirty miles per hour, it seems like you don't have any time to think. Your mind locks up and you crash. As soon as you are used to sliding at forty miles per hour, coach moves you up again, and you crash until you can handle fifty miles per hour. You literally crash your way to the top.

Once beginning sliders are finally sliding from the top of the track, if they make a mistake on curve seven, they will probably crash on curve nine, because, being inexperienced, they still have not developed a feel for the sled. They don't even realize when they have made a mistake, and even if they do, they don't know how to get out of trouble. As a result, the first couple of years on the luge really are brutal. You crash all the time, you are always bruised up and beat up, and much more likely to quit. If you can make it through the first couple of years, you are much more likely to make it all the way.

By creating a support team, it got to the point where even if I had a bad crash, a crash that really shook me up, it was going to be easier to get back on the sled than to come home and tell everyone I had quit. I couldn't quit. I just couldn't let my support team down.

By that point, the dream to be an Olympian wasn't just "my" dream any longer. This dream had become "our" dream; a dream owned by me, owned by my family, and owned by every person who was supporting me. I just happened to be the guy on the sled.

My passion about the Olympic dream attracted people to me. Everyone has the capacity to be passionate about something. Unfortunately, most people keep their passion all bottled up. They don't want to show their passion for fear of what others might think of them.

I didn't care what others thought about me or my dream. I actually wanted to know who believed in me and who didn't so I could stop associating with those who didn't. I made it a point to only spend time with my supporters. Doing so helped me become unstoppable.

The first part of leadership is passion for the cause. The second part is integrity. Integrity has to do with being a person who walks his talk; a person who does what he says. Just like there is no such thing as being a "little bit" pregnant, you can't have just a little integrity. You either have integrity or you don't.

Would you follow someone you don't trust? Of course not. By the same token, people will only follow you if they trust you, believe in you, and can count on you. Therefore, if you want to be the leader and you want others to follow you, you need to be absolutely trustworthy. Your word is Gold. You keep your word. You start being very careful about what you promise. You deliver on every promise. Every time you don't deliver, your credibility and your reputation suffer, and people stop following you. So from now on, under promise and over deliver - forever. If you become known as a person who consistently over delivers, you will stand out from the crowd. When people think about you they will think, "I can trust him" or "I can trust her."

Everyone is looking for someone to follow. Even leaders look for someone to follow. Leaders look for someone who can help them get to the next level.

People are naturally drawn to those whom they can trust; they tend to follow people who are passionate about something. Anything.

Remember the scene in the movie "Forest Gump," where Forest runs across the United States for three years? People actually started running behind him. Some of them actually thought Forest was some kind of wise man, they thought Forest was a guru. Forest wasn't a guru. Forest was just passionate about running.

If you have passion for your cause and you are a person of integrity, you'll be ahead of 95% of the people out there. People will be drawn to you, and it will be easier for you to accomplish great things.

Leadership is all about passion and integrity.

If you're excited about your objectives and people can trust you, they will follow you.

Don't Take "No" for an Answer

Once I decided on the luge, the next thing I did was to write a letter to Sports Illustrated asking "Where do you go to learn how to luge?" If you are operating from the standpoint of wishful thinking, you don't go looking for the answers. You just hope the dream will somehow fall on your lap. However, once you commit to the goal, you get hungry about finding a way to reach the goal and to make the dream happen.

Sports Illustrated actually wrote back. Their letter said, "Go to Lake Placid, New York. That's where they had the Olympics in 1936 and in 1980. That's where the track is."

I called Lake Placid and told the guy who answered the phone, "I'm an athlete in Houston. I want to learn how to luge so I can be in the Olympics in four years. Will you help me?"

You have to ask in order to get. If you don't get, you keep asking until you do get.

The guy who answered the phone said, "How old are you?"

"Twenty-one years old."

"Twenty-one? You're way too old. You're ten years too late. By now you should have ten years experience. We start them up when they're ten years old. Forget it."

I couldn't forget it. But I didn't know what to do. I didn't know how to handle his objection. All I knew was that hanging up the phone was not an option.

I believe God puts a dream in your heart. Along with that dream God gives us all the gifts, resources, and assets we'll need to make our dream a reality. It's up to us to believe that we have it within us, and once we do, it's up to us to do the work and pursue our dream. I believe God uses dreams to get us to grow into better people.

For the first time in my life I believed in myself. So I

could not hang up the phone. For all I knew, they could have hired this guy yesterday. This morning during his job orientation someone could have said to him, "Look at the juniors over there, they're only ten years old. That's where they get started" "And see that phone over there? That's where you're going to start. You'll be answering the phones around here for your first month on the job."

They have him answering the phone for the first month of his on-the-job training, and now this new hire is a professional dream stealer. A professional dream stealer backed by the whole Luge Federation.

Whenever anyone tells you that you can't do something, you're talking to a small thinker; someone who does not believe as much as you believe. Chances are, they are telling you "no" because they simply don't have the power to say "yes."

Impossible is just the opinion of somebody who does not believe as much as you do.

Whenever someone tells you "no," be polite and talk with someone a couple of levels higher. I promise you, the higher you go, the higher the belief level; and the bigger the belief level, the bigger the thinking. Remember, big people don't laugh at big ideas.

I'll let you in on a secret; a secret that's worth many times the price of this book. The higher you go up the ladder of authority, the easier the people are to speak with. People who hold positions high up in organizational chart possess better interpersonal skills or "people skills." Their people skills are a big reason they have these high positions. When you speak to them, just remember to sound confident and respect their time.

I could not hang up on this guy who had answered the phone. However, not knowing how to handle the guy's objection, I decided to tell him my life story, my dream to compete in the Olympics, and how I wanted to luge. I was stalling, buying time, until I thought of another plan to get this guy to help me.

As I told him my life story, I thought to myself, "There is always a way, there is always a way, I will find a way, because there is always a way if I don't quit."

Along the way I happened to mention having been born in Argentina. All of a sudden, the guy got all excited.

"Argentina? Why didn't you say so? If you'll compete for Argentina we'll help you."

"Why is that? A minute ago you weren't going to help me at all."

"The sport of luge," he began, "is in danger of not even being an Olympic sport in the future. There are not enough countries that compete in the luge at the International Level. We're recruiting countries."

"If you'll agree to compete for Argentina and somehow we can get you to top fifty in the world in four years, which is what you need to do to qualify for the Olympics, you would be adding one country to the sport of luge and it would make luge a stronger sport. If you qualify, you'd be helping the U.S. Team."

Big people don't laugh at big ideas.

"How's my qualifying going to help the U.S.?" I asked.

"Think about it," he said, "We're investing millions of dollars to train the U.S. Team. If the sport of luge is dropped from the Olympics, it's money down the drain. So, will you compete for Argentina?"

I thought about it, for about a nanosecond, then said, "Of course I'll compete for Argentina! I just want to be in the Olympics! I don't even care in what sport."

Back then, if Tiddlywinks had been an Olympic sport, I would have gone for Tiddlywinks. It didn't matter. I still would have been an Olympian. But, they didn't have

Olympic Tiddlywinks back then; and they still don't have it, so I competed in the luge.

The luge was just the vehicle. The Olympics was the goal, the dream, the objective. Winners focus on the objective. Not on the obstacles and the struggle they have to go through to get there.

What if I had hung up the phone when he first laughed at me? I never would have competed in the Olympics. And I would have regretted it for the rest of my life.

Do you see how important it is to "hang on?" Do you see how different doors opened? Do you see how possibilities that I never could have imagined suddenly appeared?

That's why you never quit; because as long as you don't quit, you still have a chance; that's why you have to believe that there is always a way. To believe is a choice. It's a choice that will change your life.

Then the luge guy said, "Before you come all the way to Lake Placid you have to know two things."

"What?" I said.

"Number one. If you want to do it at your age and you want to do it in only four years, it will be brutal. Brutal. Nine out of every ten people quit."

When he said that, I started smiling. "Wow! This works right into my plan!" I thought.

"O.K. What's the second thing?" I said.

"Expect to break some bones." He said.

"Greeeeeeeeeeat!!!" I shouted.

Then there was a long pause. "What do you mean great? Are you nuts? I just told you that you might break some bones."

"Look, Man." I told him, "I hope it's ten times harder than what you're saying. I hope it's a hundred times harder. The harder it is the easier it is for me. Because I'm not a quitter."

It was true. That was my only chance; that this sport, this

crazy sport of luge, had be so hard that everyone else quit. Only this way would my strength, perseverance, make a difference. Crazy logic but very logical if you think about it.

I don't think he thought I was being logical. He must have thought that I was just a cocky Texan, because he said, "Alright Hoss, come on down. Let's see what you can do." And he hung up.

What would you have done at that point? Would you have gone? Or would you have stayed home? It's so easy to quit before you even get started; so easy to do all the research and then back off… to back off and for the rest of your life bore people with your wimpy stories, your lame stories about how you tried to go to the Olympics but were unlucky. I don't have any respect people who try, only to quit when the going gets tough. I respect people who do whatever it takes for as long as it takes.

By the way, the top fifty luge athletes in the world got to go to the Olympics. If number fifty-one gave it all he had and still came up short, he's still a winner in my book. He's a winner because he took the journey, put himself through the struggle, and is now a better person for it. If number fifty-one gave it all he had, in the pursuit of his dream, he will have no regrets.

What do you do when everyone else thinks you're nuts for aspiring for more in life? What you need to do is listen to and trust your gut feelings. Trust your intuition. Your gut feeling will never steer you wrong.

It's tough to take action when you're full of fears and doubts. But once you start, once you face the fears and that gutless enemy, "doubt," you'll be better for it.

Success is all about guts and vision – knowing what you want, and having the guts to go after it.

Celebrate Every Small Victory

A few days after the phone call to Lake Placid, I was walking down Main Street, Lake Placid looking for the U.S. Olympic Training Center. I could not believe I was there, walking where all those great athletes had walked just four years earlier. I had goose bumps on top of my goose bumps.

Finally, I found it. The sign said U.S. Olympic Training Center. Back then, Olympic Center was at the old Marcy Hotel on Main Street. A few years later, the U.S. Olympic Committee built a world-class Training Center on some acreage outside of town. It was so exciting to be there standing outside the OTC. I opened up my bag, pulled my camera out, tossed it to a passerby and asked him to take my picture right there!

Lake Placid 1984

Walking inside the building I started meeting some of the athletes; boxers, runners, kayakers, bobsledders. Being there was so exciting that it felt like I had just died and gone to Heaven.

One of the athletes mentioned that we were only two blocks from the hockey arena where the Americans had beaten the Russians in the Miracle Game of the 1980 Winter Olympics.

"You're kidding me right? You're pulling my leg!" I said.

"I'm serious, the ice arena is two block away," he said.

The excitement was so overwhelming, that I didn't even check into my room. Leaving my bags with the receptionist, I bolted out the door to go and see the place where those heroes of mine had overcome such great odds to win.

I ran over to the arena and could not believe I was there. Even though the arena was empty, it was magical just to be there. I could almost see those hockey players fighting for the puck. I could still feel the energy from that incredible night four years earlier. I stayed in the arena for over an hour, walking through every section and soaking up that energy; the energy of my heroes who had overcome and won. I would need that energy in the next four years.

A couple of blocks further down the street, I walked into the Olympic Skating Oval where Eric Heiden won his five Olympic speed skating medals. Eric Heiden was another miracle athlete. What he did was unheard of. Heiden won the gold medal in the sprint, middle distance, and long distance events. It's as if Carl Lewis had won the 100 meter dash, the 10,000 meter race, and the marathon. Slowly walking around the Olympic oval, I could almost see Heiden swooshing by in his yellow speed suit.

I was on my way to fully realizing my dream, excited every step of the way. You need to get excited every step of the way, too. You need to celebrate every small victory on the road to your dream because the road to your dream is a long and arduous one. Celebrating your victories puts you in a powerful state of mind that makes you stronger for the road ahead.

Before leaving Houston for Lake Placid, something happened that helped me make my Olympic dream a reality.

The Principles of Success

One of my friends is a very successful business owner. My friend asked me to meet with him at his office before I left for Lake Placid. His office was way across town which is an hour's drive across Houston's bumper-to-bumper traffic. I was willing to drive across Houston because I respected my friend's experience and knowledge.

People that succeed in business, school, the Olympics, or in life, follow the same set of rules. These rules are called Principles of Success. By definition, Principles of Success will work for anyone, anywhere, anytime. They are timeless principles that are thousands of years old. They are the distilled wisdom of the ages.

When I finally arrived at his office, my friend said, "Ruben, never forget: Rule Number One in success is to never quit. As long as you don't quit, you still have a chance."

I told my friend, "You made me drive across Houston for that? I know that! I've been living it all my life. I'm Bulldog, remember?"

He smiled, and said "Even 'Bulldogs' need to be reminded of that sometimes. Here's my business card. Take it with you to Lake Placid. If you're having a bad day at the track, give me a call. I'll get you back on the sled."

I took the card, put it in my pocket, thanked him, and as I was leaving, I remember thinking, "I'm not going to have to call you," my cocky twenty-one year-old thinking on full tilt. Later, I realized that that mind-set was not very smart, because once I got to Lake Placid and started training, I was calling him every night.

The Driving Force
Behind Success

At Lake Placid, I was placed in the beginner luge class with fourteen other "aspiring Olympians." We were training in the old bobsled track, a mean concrete track that was filled with wicked turns.

We trained on wheeled sleds at fifty miles per hour. We wore tennis shoes, shorts, a t-shirt and a crash helmet. The helmet is just for decoration, because if you crashed, you went straight to the hospital. That's the weeding out process in the sport of luge. I guess the coaches want to know right away if you're serious or not.

Everyone thinks lugers are all thrill seekers. The nuts, the thrill seekers, and the daredevils don't last. Those guys are just in it for the adrenaline rush. They don't have any staying power. The guys who last, the ones who make it, are the analytical ones. The ones that understand that luge is a means to an end: The Olympics.

Out of all the sports I've ever played, the luge had the biggest concentration of PhD's and scientists. The luge attracts analytical types: authors, professors, doctors, engineers, and lawyers can be found in the luge circuit. I'm very analytical. I have degrees in Chemistry and Biology. If I can graph it, I can understand it.

Lugers are an analytical bunch; not the crowd of characters you might expect a sport like this to attract. But you know what? When you read Chuck Yeager's biography, Yeager explains that the best test pilots were not the daredevils. The best test pilots were the very analytical engineer types who had the brains and guts. Either one of these characteristics alone is not great; but together, they make a great combination.

I'll never forget my first luge run. I was so pumped up. I remember thinking to myself, "I'm not a groupie anymore. I'm on the road to the Olympics!" At the bottom of the track they didn't even give us a ride back up. We had to carry our sleds back up the track. But it didn't matter. I was on cloud nine.

The coaches made it difficult on us purposely. They wanted to know right away how badly we wanted it. They didn't want to waste any time with anyone who was not serious.

If you've ever played football, you know exactly what I mean. The first couple of weeks of football practice each season are brutal. The coach works the players to death because he wants to find out who his real team will be. He wants to cull out all the wanna-bees. They do the same thing in military boot camp.

There are many facets to success. You have to have a dream – not just any dream; a dream that takes your breath away; a dream that you're willing to fight for. You have to believe in yourself. You have to take massive action with singleness of purpose. And finally, you have to have the attitude that you are willing to do whatever it takes for as long as it takes. Then, and only then, is success realistic.

More than anything else, your desire will determine if you will make it. Napoleon Hill said, "Desire is the starting point of all achievement, not a hope, not a wish, but a keen pulsating desire which transcends everything."

How badly do you want it? Is your dream something that you'd like to do? Is it something that would be nice to do? Or is it something that you are obsessed about; something that you must do?

Your desire will determine whether you'll realize your dream because how badly you want something determines what will make you quit. Burning desire allows a person with average ability to successfully compete with those who have far more ability.

Desire allows you to give it everything you've got. It helps you reach your full potential. Intense desire allows people to win against overwhelming odds.

If your dream is not an obsession, as soon as you come across obstacles, you'll quit. Weak desires produce weak results because as soon as the challenge of reaching your dream becomes an inconvenience, you'll give up.

As long as you don't quit, you still have a chance.

Success is not convenient. Trust me. In order to succeed you will need to inconvenience yourself in a big way – for a long time. That's why it's so important to be driven, excited, and passionate about your dream. If your "why?" is big enough, the "how" will take care of itself.

So, there I was, carrying my sled back up the mountain after my first wheeled luge run ever. Since it was summertime, there were a few tourists watching us train. As I was walking back up the track after my first run, I remember coming face to face with an older man who had just seen me slide down the mountain. Our eyes met and I told him, serious as a heart attack, "I'm going to be in the Olympics in four years."

He looked at me, paused, and then said, "Son, I think you're going to make it. I can see the passion in your eyes."

Can people see the passion in your eyes when you tell them about your plans, dreams and aspirations? How do you expect others to get excited about your goals, dreams and projects if you're not excited about them?

The more passionate and enthusiastic you are about

your dreams, the more others will believe in you and the more followers you'll attract. Your passion will breed the conviction you'll need to turn mediocrity into excellence. Your passion will help you overcome any circumstance and help you become unstoppable.

We all have the capacity to get passionate. Unfortunately most of us keep our enthusiasm bottled up. It's like emotional constipation.

After all, what if you told someone about your dreams and they laughed at you? Or even worse, what if they didn't laugh and you didn't reach your dream? That would not feel good, would it? Who cares? Be enthusiastic anyways. Having small thinkers laugh at you is part of the price of success. Do you want to be mediocre or do you want to be great? To be great is to be misunderstood.

How to Develop
An Unstoppable Will

As soon as I returned to my room after my first day of luge training, I called my businessman-friend.

"Craig. This is nuts! My side hurts. I think I broke my foot. That's it. I'm going back to soccer!"

Craig interrupted me, "Ruben, get in front of a mirror!"

"What?"

"I said to get in front of a mirror!"

I stretched the phone cord and stood in front of a full length mirror.

"Now repeat after me. No matter how bad it is, and how bad it gets, I'm going to make it!"

I felt like an idiot staring at myself in the mirror. In the most wimpy, wishy-washy way possible, I said, "No matter how bad it is, and how bad it gets, I'm going to make it!"

"C'mon! Say it right. You're Mr. Olympic Man! That's all you ever talk about! Are you going to do it or not?"

I got serious, "No matter how bad it is, and how bad it gets, I'm going to make it!"

"Again! Louder!

"No matter how bad it is, and how bad it gets, I'm going to make it!"

And again and again and again I said it over and over.

The first time I said it, I felt like an idiot. After repeating the phrase five times, I thought, "Hey, I'm feeling kind of good. I'm standing a little bit straighter."

After saying it ten times, I jumped up in the air and shouted, "I don't care what happens. I'm going to make it. I can break both legs. Bones heal. I'll come back and I will make it. I will be an Olympian!"

That was when I became an Olympian in my mind. That's when I burned all the bridges and became totally committed to my dream. Right there and then, I made a decision that from that point on, I was going to treat a broken bone like a temporary inconvenience. A broken bone was not going to make me quit. It was not even going to affect my attitude. It was only going to make me tougher inside. You have to learn to meet hard times with a harder will.

Burning desire creates the power to succeed.

It's amazing what happens to your self belief when you get eyeball to eyeball with yourself and you forcibly tell yourself what you're going to accomplish. It's amazing. You've got to try it…. only wait until everyone leaves your home before doing it. Otherwise they'll think you're nuts.

Paying the Price of Success

A funny thing started happening. Everyday, there were less people showing up for practice. They were actually quitting on their dream. I couldn't believe it. Maybe they didn't want it as badly as I did. Maybe they were not smart enough to call someone when they were struggling. I don't know why they quit.

They all had great reasons for quitting. They rationalized it real well. "It's too hard. It's too cold. It's too expensive. I miss my family. I don't like the luge."

I didn't like the luge either! I was killing myself out there. But I was willing to do it regardless of the costs. Why? Because the luge was the vehicle to my Olympic dream.

How badly you want something determines what you are willing to do to get it. Weak desires produce weak results.

Whenever you rationalize something, you're just saying something that sounds good. A rationalization is telling yourself a rational lie.

Four years and a few broken bones later, I was walking into the Opening Ceremonies of the 1988 Calgary Winter Olympics. I felt so happy, so proud; but at the same time I was feeling sad for the ones who had quit. After all, what were they feeling now?

The ones who had quit along the way were watching the Olympics on TV. I'll bet they felt sick inside. I'll bet it hurt so much that they had to change channels. I'll bet they can't watch the Olympics for the rest of their lives.

The regret must be eating them up. I'll bet every time they think about the Olympics they ask themselves, "What if I hadn't quit?" On their deathbed they'll be thinking, "What

Racing at the 1988 Calgary Winter Olympics

if?" Their decision to quit will haunt them forever.

I paid a huge price to make it to the Olympics. Everyone will pay a huge price for success. The price of success is non-negotiable. But the price of regret is hundreds of times bigger. So you might as well go for success so you can make your life an adventure.

Which will you choose: immediate gratification or long term success? The quality of your life hinges on that choice. Which will it be? It's your choice.

You'll either pay the price of success or the price of regret.

The price of success weighs ounces. The price of regret weighs tons.

It's Your Choice.

PART TWO

How to Become Unstoppable

1992 Albertville Olympic Luge Ticket

*"If one advances confidently in
the direction of his dreams,
he will meet with a success
unexpected in common hours."*

- Henry David Thoreau

How to Discover Your Dream and Purpose

When you're not doing what you're supposed to be doing in your life, it's just like when you are writing with the wrong hand. You can do it, and after a while you can get pretty good at it, but it's always awkward. But when you find what you're supposed to do with your life, it's like putting the pen back in the hand where it belongs.

Many times after speaking at a convention or a corporate event someone will approach me and ask, "How do you figure out what your dream is?"

It all comes down to spending some quality time getting to know yourself through some very specific questions. Go out by yourself for a couple of days to a quiet place, maybe a cabin in the woods, out by a lake, a place where you will not be interrupted and spend some quality time really thinking about your dream. It might be a good idea to take a notebook with you so you can write your thoughts.

The experiences you have had up to this point in your life have prepared you for your life purpose. You have unique talents, abilities, interests, and values that only you can bring to greatness. There is a destiny that only you can fulfill. But first you need to find out what you would love to do. What you would be willing to do for free. What you are good at doing. What is extremely important to you. What you were born to do.

Some of your most important dreams had their beginnings in your childhood. What did you dream about then? It's never too late to make your childhood dreams come true.

The secret to a successful life is to find your destiny and then do it.

Below are some questions to help you get started. Don't just glance at them. Invest some time in them. Remember, what you learn from these questions could change your life. Get a notebook, write one each of these questions on top of each page. Then, spend at least fifteen minutes on each one. Invest just fifteen minutes writing your unique answers in your life mission notebook.

Remember, there are no wrong answers. This is just an exercise to help you find your true North.

What are some of my greatest talents?

What do others say I am good at?

What do others say that makes me unique?

What have my unique life experiences
    prepared me to do?

What do I love to do so much that I would do it for free?

What are my hobbies?

What would I be willing to die for? Why?

Where have I excelled in the past?

What is important to me?

What do I naturally do well?

What do I feel called to do?

What excites me about life? Why?

What do I daydream about doing? Why?

What things do I want to be remembered for
at the end of my life?

If I had a year left to live, what would I do differently?

What would I do if I knew I could not fail? Why?

What would I do with my time if I were wealthy?

Where can I make a difference?

How do I want to be remembered? Why?

What legacy do I want to leave behind? Why?

Remember, you can't make your dream come true if you don't even know what it is. If you can't see it, you can't get it. Once you see it, and you dedicate your life to making it a reality, your life will become more meaningful, because life changes with the knowledge that you are going somewhere.

"Destiny is not a matter of chance;
it is a matter of choice.
It is not something to be waited for;
but, rather something to be achieved."

- William Jennings Bryan

How to Use Your Creativity to Win More in Life

Most people go through life making decisions based on just a fraction of their available options. They hold themselves back because they allow circumstances or other people's opinions to limit their perceived choices.

My great-great grandparents lived in Torino, Italy. At the turn of the century they took a huge risk. They left everything behind and moved to Argentina looking for a better life. They settled in a small dairy town of about a thousand people and created a better life for themselves.

My grandmother grew up in the same small town. In this town, everyone thought they had only two career options: working at the dairy bottling factory, or working at the farm raising dairy cattle. Grandma was more adventurous. Rather than stay in her native town, Grandma took a chance, moved to a big city, married a restaurateur, and lived her dream.

My Dad was a chemical engineer in a small oil town. In 1968, when economic and social conditions started to deteriorate in Argentina, rather than stay there, he took a chance and moved with my mom, my brother, and I to the U.S. Leaving his friends and family in search for more opportunity was a risky and scary move, especially since he didn't speak much English back then, but in the long run it really paid off.

We lived in Houston, Texas for over 30 years. I could never get used to the heat and humidity. In 2010 we moved to Colorado Springs and absolutely love it here (I jokingly tell my audiences that if my great-great-grandparents had simply moved to Colorado, we would all have saved a lot of time).

The Jamaican bobsledders did the same thing. They were originally world-class sprinters. When they didn't qualify for the Summer Olympics in track and field, they decided to get creative. Deciding to take up the bobsled was sheer genius. They didn't just take the road less traveled. They paved a brand new road where there had been no road before. Everyone who makes fun of them has no clue about what it really takes to succeed in life.

I'm amazed when people ask me how someone from hot and humid Houston can compete in the luge. It's really quite simple. I came to the realization that the city I live in has nothing to do with what sport I compete in. When the first cold front hits Houston, I fly out to the luge tracks. The luge tracks have never come nor will they ever come to me.

Start looking outside your immediate surroundings for ways to realize your dream. Don't limit your options to what's obvious. Get a little creative, take a chance, and do something different. Chase your dream. Your dream will not land on your lap. You have to go out and get it. When you start getting bold and unconventional, your life will become an adventure and you'll be a lot more successful.

"You can steer the course you choose in the direction of where you want to be."

- W. Clement Stone

"The world will make room for the man whose words and actions show that he knows where he is going."

- Napoleon Hill

How to Use Goals to Get what You Desire

A couple of weeks after I wrote Sports Illustrated asking them where you go to learn how to luge, they sent me an 8x10 photograph of a guy racing on a luge. As soon as I got the picture, I framed it and hung it up in my room right in front of my bed.

Every morning, the first person I saw when I woke up was "The Luge Man." Seeing "The Luge Man" was a constant reminder that I was training for the Olympics. He reminded me to eat right, to work out, and to surround myself with winners. At night, before turning out the lights, the last person I saw was "The Luge Man." All night long, I dreamt about the luge and the Olympics.

During the day, the picture focused my conscious mind on the dream. At night, it conditioned my unconscious mind to aim for my goal.

It's important to keep reminders of your goals in front of you all the time. The walls of my office are completely covered with Olympic memorabilia: posters, awards, medals, pictures of the luge tracks, even a huge Olympic flag signed by all my heroes. All of them are reminders of my dream and mind-builders towards my goal.

By doing this, my mind is constantly bombarded with my dream, competing in the Winter Olympic Games. No matter where I look, I'm continually reminded of where I

"The Luge Man"

am headed, where I want to go. If I daydream, I daydream about the Olympics.

I always carry CDs with Olympic music in my car. I actually listened to a CD of the Salt Lake City Opening Ceremonies on the way to the gym to get myself all fired up.

In order to make big goals possible, many things have to happen simultaneously. Therefore, you can't afford to rely on chance. You do everything humanly possible to make the different factors happen – to orchestrate events to put yourself position yourself to win. For example, to get to the Olympics I had to set financial goals, conditioning goals, technical training goals, and organizational goals.

Back in 1984, reaching my financial goal was pretty simple. The length of my luge season was determined by how much money I had saved all year. As soon as I ran out of money, it was time to go home. At the time, I was still living at home with my parents, so my expenses were minimal. But not having any sponsors, I had to save every penny I made. Back then, when I went on a date, we didn't even go to the dollar movie, we waited until Tuesday night when it was fifty cents.

Conditioning goals were also fairly simple. I would simply follow my coaches' advice. Unlike most Olympic athletes, I worked out on my own – I couldn't afford personal trainers. But my coaches gave me a training plan, and I provided the willingness to follow it.

Learning the technical aspect of luge – how to drive the different tracks – was fairly simple (simple as in a few steps; but not easy to physically master).

My technical success depended on listening to my coaches. We would break each track into sections; break sections down to the curves; and, finally, we would learn exactly how to steer each section of every curve.

Then, just like airline pilots, we were required to know what to do if something went wrong. For example, if you enter a curve a little too late, you need to, immediately, make a correction or else you could crash a couple of curves later.

Over a period of years, I slowly developed a "feel," a feeling, a familiarity, of my "space" as I came down the track. The most experienced lugers have developed their "feel" so much; that they are able to slide blindly, with their head tucked back, in order to be that much more aerodynamic.

It was challenging to meet my financial requirements, my conditioning goals, and my luge technique goals. But, by taking full responsibility, I had full control. In other words, I had only myself to blame if I didn't produce.

Unfortunately, there was one piece of the puzzle that was not under my control; one piece where I had to do everything I could on faith and then pray that everything would work out.

In order to even have a chance to qualify for the Olympics, I had to start racing internationally by the end of my second season. Even if you qualify for a World Cup race, they will not let you race unless your country has a National Luge

Federation that is recognized by its Olympic Committee and by the International Luge Federation.

I was pioneering the sport of luge for Argentina. Obviously, Argentina didn't have a luge federation. If I wanted to race internationally, it was going to be up to me to create an Argentine Luge Federation and I was going to have to do it from Houston.

Imagine that. There I was, just learning the sport, and I had to convince the Argentines that, in just four years, I would be good enough to qualify for the Olympics. Mustering the belief that I could convince them, was the toughest hurdle I had to face on the way to the Olympics. It was a huge mental hurdle because the chances of it actually happening were so remote that it almost made no sense to even go for it.

If my desire to become an Olympian had not been so great, I would not have gone for it. But, I wanted it so badly that I figured, "If I don't give it all I have, I'll only regret it later."

Once the decision was made, I just set a goal to do everything in my power to make it happen. For two years, while learning how to luge, my Dad and I wrote countless letters to the Argentine Olympic Committee asking them to form a Luge Federation.

We wrote a lot of letters. A lot of letters. I have a three-inch-thick, three ring binder filled with copies of the letters. And we didn't just hit them with quantity. We hit them with quality. Our letters were not filled with fluff. They were filled with all kinds of data and graphs that showed my progress.

Having no personal credibility, I decided to use the best credibility in the world. I asked the U.S. Olympic Luge Team coaches to write letters for me and to include progress reports on how my training was going. The Argentines would have been nuts to listen to me, but they could not ignore the U.S. Olympic Luge Team coaches.

God honors commitment. Just like clockwork, a couple

of weeks before our deadline, the Argentine Olympic Committee decided to create a Luge Federation. The International Luge Federation gave their approval and I was on my way.

The next time you are working on a big goal, do what I did: break it down into manageable chunks. In so doing, you will see those challenges in a different light which can help you muster up the courage, the gumption to take action. Inch by inch; life's a cinch; yard by yard, it's hard.

At the Olympic Training Center we are taught about the importance of writing down our goals every day. Magic happens when you write down goals. Writing out your goals is an act of commitment. When you write out your goals, you are actually writing the script to the story of your future.

The coaches taught us to take a 3x5 card and to write our goals on it in a certain, special way. On one side of the card, write your goal in the present tense – as if the goal is already happening. On the other side write three things that you are doing every day to make your goal a reality.

My latest Olympic goal card said, "It's February 2010, I'm walking into the Opening Ceremony of the Vancouver Winter Olympics. I am a four-time Olympian." The back of my card said, "I'm a four-time Olympian because: I work out every day, I eat right, I hang around winners, and I'm willing to do whatever it takes for as long as it takes.

Yes, there are four things on the back of my goal card. I wanted to have a spare tire just in case. The front side of the card reminds you of where you're going. The back side fuels your belief because your subconscious starts thinking, "I'm doing the work, therefore, it's just a matter of time before my goal becomes a reality."

Eventually you get to the point where you start believing you deserve it. When you have worked so hard that you start believing you deserve it, you start developing the unstoppable attitude of winners.

Some people will tell you to put the goal card in your wallet, to carry it with you wherever you go, and to read it five times a day. Don't. If you put the card in your wallet, next time you see it will be five years from now when you buy a new wallet.

Don't carry it in your wallet. Instead, tape the card to the mirror in your bathroom right where you brush your teeth. Read your goals first thing in the morning and last thing at night. The best time to read your goals is when you're half asleep.

That's when your mind is most easily conditioned. Read them with passion – like you're mad. As you read your goals, look at yourself in the mirror. Lock into your eyeballs. That's how you read your goals if you're serious about them.

Goal setting works because it gives you direction. Goals remind you of where you're going. They give your life focus and keep you from wasting your time. As soon as you set a goal, your mind starts trying to figure out a way to reach the goal.

People that don't set goals are aimless wanderers. They are usually bored and not as happy as people who have a clear, defined purpose. When life seems to be lacking purpose, many people fill their days with diversions to distract them from the gnawing ache of emptiness in their heart. Diversions like watching too much TV, spending too much time aimlessly surfing the net, or drinking too much are simply modern anesthesia to dull the pain. If they would just get honest with themselves, search deep inside for that childhood dream, and set out on a quest for it, their lives would instantly become more meaningful and the dull pain would be replaced with excitement and joy.

You must be crystal clear about your goals and about when you will achieve them. For example, writing, "By July 26, I will weigh 195 pounds," works much better than writing, "I need to lose some weight."

It's not hard to get specific about your goals. Every time you step into your car, I'll bet you know precisely where you are going. You have a destination in mind. You have purpose. You have just set a specific goal.

You don't step into your car thinking, "I don't know where I'm going. I guess I'll just drive around and see where I wind up." At least I hope you don't.

America was built on dreams, but believe it or not, a huge percentage of the people in the United States, arguably the most goal-oriented nation in the world, live their whole lives just like that – as aimless wanderers. They've dropped out of life, they've dropped out of their basic responsibilities, and they've dropped out of productive competition. They're the people who avoid difficult tasks and grab on to the first job they are offered, clinging to it like frightened leeches for the rest of their unproductive lives. They live their whole lives without meaning or inspiration. They don't live life, they simply exist.

That's why it's really not that hard to become a high-achiever. It's just a decision. Once you make a quality decision to commit to do whatever it takes to realize your dream, once you decide quitting is not an option, before long you'll be on top. There is no competition. The only competition is your willingness to commit to your dream. So let others live small lives. Let others leave their lives in someone else's hands. But not you.

David Jensen, the Chief Administrative Officer for the Crump Institute for Biological Imaging, UCLA School of Medicine, conducted a goal-setting study of a group of people from a cross-section of occupations; doctors to businessmen, to truck drivers. These were actually people who had paid money to attend Zig Ziglar seminars. So we're talking about a group of people who were willing to invest in themselves to achieve more in life.

The researchers found that the people who had created

a goal program earned twice as much as those who hadn't. But that's not all. They were also happier, healthier, and had better relationships with their family members. The bottom line is that the people who had taken the time to develop goal plans for their lives were enjoying their lives much more than the people who were leaving their lives to chance.

Goals give your life direction and help you have more control of your life and more peace of mind. So what are you waiting for? Take a little time and put together a goals program for your life. It's not that hard. A good start would be to answer the following questions...

What, specifically would you like to achieve? What would achieving your goal mean for you? Can you get emotional about achieving your goal? Do you have a burning desire? What do you need to overcome to achieve your goal? What resources do you need? Who can help you along the way? What new skills do you need to develop? What is your plan for making it happen? When do you want to reach your goal? Decide to create a goals program and watch your life change.

Set goals. If you're not headed somewhere in life, you're headed nowhere.

"Every time I play, in my own mind I'm the favorite."

- Tiger Woods

A Proven Technique
Every Champion Uses

There is something that every professional athlete, Olympic athlete, professional golfer, astronaut, and every top achiever does to win more often. They use a technique called visualization.

Visualization is just a fancy word for "vividly imagining" what it will feel like when you reach your goal. What will it look like? What will it sound like? What will it smell like? What will it taste like? What will it feel like? Visualization is your mind's sneak preview of coming attractions. It's a mental blueprint of your future.

While training for my first Olympics, I might have been jogging, lifting weights, eating dinner, or simply walking in the mall, but you know what was going on in my head?

In my mind, I was walking into the Opening Ceremonies, the crowd was cheering wildly, to the right I could see the Olympic Flag waving, behind me I could see the Olympic Torch, I could hear the orchestra playing the Olympic Anthem – my favorite song in the whole wide world. I was there! High-fiving my teammates shouting, "We made it guys! We made it! It was worth it! We're Olympians!" I could feel the cold wind blowing on my face, the snow hitting my face, the tears of joy running down my cheeks and the goose bumps running up my neck, my cheeks, my forehead. I was there!

And four years later, when I was actually walking into

the Opening Ceremonies, it was just like when I'd imagined it. Only a hundred times better.

The mind cannot tell the difference between something you are vividly imagining with all your senses, heart, and passion, and something that is actually happening. By regularly picturing what you intend to do, you become like a guided missile that can't miss its target. You rekindle the flame of belief and literally become unstoppable.

There are miracles with your name on them. Miracles you were created to go out and make happen; miracles that are just waiting for you to heed the call; waiting for you to dare to take the journey to achieve them.

By constantly seeing your miracle in your mind's eye, you will strengthen the belief and the desire you need to make the journey. Do this, and success will be a matter of time.

Note - To watch a short video of the visualization process, visit FourWinterGames.com or RubenTV.com.

There are miracles with your name on them. Success is yours for the taking, if you will only believe.

"I never did anything by accident, nor did any of my inventions come indirectly by accident."

- Thomas Edison

Game Plans
for Success

Everyone wants to win. Wanting to win is not enough. You have to be willing to prepare to win. No matter how many times we've been to a particular track, before we train on it we "walk the track" with Coach.

A typical week during the World Cup circuit is like this: Tuesday through Friday we take our training and qualifying runs; Saturday and Sunday we race; and Mondays are for traveling to the next track.

Within Europe, we drive from track to track in vans. For races outside of Europe we fly. No matter how long we have been traveling, no matter of how tired we are, whether we've just ridden in a van for twelve hours from Innsbruck to Sarajevo, or flown ten hours from Europe to Calgary, before we go to the hotel we walk the track.

We go to the top of the track and for two hours we literally walk down the track, slipping and sliding the whole way, planning exactly what lines we will take during training. Coach knows the best lines – he was World Champion three times. Coach knows the shortcut to success. We follow Coach and take detailed notes on everything he says.

Typically it goes something like this; "O.K. guys, this is curve three. You want to enter early. At this point you want to be no more than three inches from the left wall. Over here steer with a force of three (where zero is no steering and ten

Walking the track in Sarajevo, Yugoslavia.

is all you've got). Down there at the expansion joint give it a five, over there by that sign hold it up, then at the end crank it with all you've got but remember to counter steer or else you'll slam into the wall."

Or Coach might say, "Take a close look at the shape of the ice at the exit of curve eleven. It's not shaped right. Notice how there's a small bump here. Be prepared for the bump. Don't let it catch you off-guard."

We feverishly write every word he says. Some of us even record Coach as he's talking. When we finally get to the hotel we don't go straight to bed; we memorize the fastest lines and start visualizing our perfect run.

What if, on the way to the track I had told Coach, "Coach, I'm not feeling well, will you just drop me off at the hotel?"

You know what would happen? I'd take a hot shower, get a hot meal, snuggle under the warm covers, watch "Friends" or "Frazier" on TV in Serbo-Croatian while sipping a hot chocolate, and drift into a wonderful night's sleep, all the while thinking, "Those fools. They're freezing their rear ends out there!" And then the next day I'd kill myself on the track, and have only myself to blame.

Wanting to win is not enough. You have to prepare to

win. Winners do whatever it takes to get to the next level. They take the time to plan ahead, and prepare to win by organizing their resources so they can accomplish their goals – regardless of the odds. Are you willing to do whatever it takes? If you're not, then your dream is a pipe-dream.

Wanting to win is not enough. You have to be willing to prepare to win.

"You have to train your mind like you train your body."

- Bruce Jenner

How to Condition
Your Mind to Succeed

Top achievers in every field understand that words have the power to condition the mind to succeed or fail. Whenever you say something, your mind tries to build a case for it. If you call yourself "stupid" the mind does a subconscious "Google search" on the word stupid and pulls up a list of every stupid thing you've ever done in your life. Armed with that list, you have the proof that you are stupid and you start acting that way. If you call yourself a winner, your mind pulls up all your winning moments. And you start acting like a winner.

In fact, if you are not getting the results you want out of life, it can probably be traced to your self talk. What you say to yourself will influence what you think. What you think influences what you do. What you do all the time becomes your habits and your habits determine your results and ultimately, your destiny.

That's why you have to be very careful with whom you associate. You don't want to get any "second hand" negative talk from the people you hang around with.

At the Olympic Training Center, they will not tolerate anyone bad-mouthing themselves. They want to create an environment conducive to achieving peak performance; an atmosphere where success is in the air. If they catch you bad-mouthing yourself, it's pushups time. Why do you think

Olympic athletes are in such great shape?

Seriously though, sometimes, even Olympic athletes forget to watch their self-talk. My worst luge crash ever was a result of negative self-talk.

One year before the Salt Lake City Olympics, we were in St. Moritz, Switzerland training for a world cup race. We were training in the morning and the Italians were training in the afternoon. At the time, the Italians were the best. So that afternoon, I went to the track to watch the Italians train. I wanted to see what lines they took down the track. I wanted to learn from the best.

I went to the fastest point of the track, curve thirteen. Watching the Italians rocket down the track at over eighty-five miles per hour was unbelievable. Every time an Italian luger went by I would mutter to myself, "I can't believe I do that." Another luge would barrel down the track and I'd say to myself, "I can't believe I do that." For two hours, I said it over and over.

Up to that day, I had not had any major problems at that track. I was just looking for a way to take my abilities to the next level - just looking to fine tune.

The next day, on my first run, as I reached Curve thirteen, my mind reminded me, "That's right, Ruben, you can't do that." And I froze; forgot to steer and had a horrible crash. I broke my foot, broke my hand, and totaled my sled. End of season.

That was the lowest point of my luge career. At that point I didn't know how I would be able to go to the Olympics. I was hurt and I could not afford another sled, and it was all because a couple of hours of negative self-talk.

I had a pity party for a couple of days but eventually, flying back home from Europe, halfway over the Atlantic, I got my head straight. I took a piece of paper and wrote, "This has been the worst year of my life; the most stressful and frustrating. I am being tested. I will pass the test. I have

St. Moritz - Broken hand, broken foot, totaled sled.

an opportunity to make an incredible comeback and show what I'm made up of." Then, I started saying to myself, "There is always a way. There is always a way. There is always a way. I will find a way, because there is always a way."

Repeating the phrase, "There is always a way," over and over, when you are facing obstacles, puts your mind in a solution-finding state. It helps you shift your focus away from the problem and into finding a solution.

And I did find a solution. I could not afford to buy another sled, but maybe I could borrow a sled. I started calling some of my best luge buddies and my good friend Adam Cook of the New Zealand Luge Team, loaned me his sled to qualify and race in the Salt Lake Olympics.

Next time you experience a major setback, do what top achievers do. Do whatever you can to recover quickly. Bouncing back is not enough. Winners bounce back quickly. They take their hit, they experience their setback, they have the wind taken out of their sails, but they focus on recovering quickly.

Right away, they force themselves to look at the bright side of things – any bright side, and they say to themselves, "That's O.K. There is always a way. I will find a way." They dust themselves off, and pick up where they left off.

The reason quick recovery is important is that if you recover quickly, you don't lose your momentum and your drive. Winners can't afford the luxury of wallowing in their misery. Winners can't afford to play the martyr. Because the moment you shift your focus from the dream to the struggle, you're dead in the water.

If you have a long pity party where you feel sorry for yourself, you will lose your mental edge, you'll lose your "Eye of the Tiger" and it will be harder to come back.

When a boxer gets knocked down, he has only ten seconds to get back up. If he gets up in eleven seconds, he loses the fight. Remember that the next time you get knocked down.

Next time life knocks you down, make a decision to dig deep inside and to find a solution. Winners always look for the solution. Losers always look for an escape.

Next time you get knocked down, decide you will act like a winner. Get up quickly, take action, and astound the world.

Don't quit on the one yard line. Play full out, follow through, and reach your goals.

"Nobody stands taller than those willing to stand corrected."

- William Safire

How to Benefit
from Other
People's Success

My first time to Lake Placid was in the spring of 1984; right after watching the Sarajevo Winter Olympics on TV. We trained for a few weeks on wheels (the wheel training was done to learn the fundamentals of steering a luge). Later that year, in the winter of 1984, I returned to Lake Placid for my first ice training. Luging on ice is completely different from luging on wheels. On ice there is hardly any traction, therefore, ice luge is much more unforgiving. It's like the difference between walking and ice skating.

When you are first learning how to luge on ice, the coaches have you slide from the bottom third of the track; where you're only traveling at about thirty miles per hour. As your skill improves, they slowly move you up the track. It takes about 100 runs before the coaches will let you slide from the top of the track.

My goal for my first luge season back in the winter of 1984 was to be able to luge from the Men's Start at the top of the track, by the end of the season. My goal for my second season, was to qualify to race in the Lake Placid World Cup.

My plan for the second season was to spend all winter in Placid, take as many runs as possible, and see if I could qualify for the race that was to be held on February 1986.

As soon as I got to Lake Placid my coaches set me straight. They said, "If you stay here all winter, your progress will be very slow. If you want to progress fast, you need to be constantly challenged. If you train at any track for more than two weeks, you'll get bored. Once you get bored you stop improving. You need to train here for two weeks, then two weeks on each of several tracks in Europe, then come back to Lake Placid and you'll be a whole second faster."

What they were telling me made absolutely no sense to me. How could training in Europe possibly improve my times in Lake Placid? It just didn't make any sense. But I'd promised myself that I would submit to my coaches' leadership and not question them. I had promised myself that I would take all of their advice on faith. After all, who was I to question the U.S. Olympic Coaches?

That season I trained in Europe. I learned different things from every track. And when I returned to Placid I was a full second faster than before. The people who didn't listen and stayed in Lake Placid all season never caught up.

Research done by Dr. W. Edwards Deming reveals that 94% of all failures occur when a person is not following a proven system. That explains why franchises have such a low failure rate. It's because they have developed a system and they follow it to a T. If you want to increase your success rate and speed up your learning curve, do yourself a favor. Find a mentor who has done what you aspire to do and then faithfully follow their advice. Follow their system. You'll be glad you did.

"He that walks with wise men shall be wise."

The Bible - Proverbs

"Everything can be taken from a man except one thing: the last of the human freedoms – to choose one's attitude in any given set of circumstances, to choose one's own way."

- Viktor Frankl

How to Think Like a Champion

What would you do if you knew you could not fail?

Back when I took up the sport of luge, one of my Olympic coaches used to tell me, "Ruben, you're only six inches away from massive success." I wasn't sure what he meant. He explained, "Six inches is the distance between your ears. Your success depends on what you feed your mind." He was talking about the "Inner Game." It would be years before I really understood what he meant. Today, I realize that he was 100% right.

You always hear about the mental part of sports being more important than the physical part. I have to admit that I was always a bit skeptical. That is, until a cold morning in October 1998.

I took up the sport of luge in 1984 and retired from the luge right after the 1992 Albertville Olympics. After Albertville, I didn't take a luge run for six years. However, during those six years I read hundreds of books on success and listened to thousands of motivational audio programs. By doing that, I was growing inside and gradually becoming mentally tougher.

In 1998, six years after retiring from the luge, I decided to begin training for the 2002 Salt Lake City Olympics. My first day of training was unforgettable. I was at the start of the Calgary luge track ready to take my first run in six years.

Surprisingly, I was feeling cool, calm, and confident. Believe it or not, my first four runs were personal bests. I felt more in control of the sled than ever before. Four personal bests after a six year break! Unbelievable! That day I stopped being a skeptic. That day I became a believer in the power of the human mind.

High achievers in every field share certain beliefs that give them a competitive edge; beliefs designed to keep them hungry, confident, and mentally tough so they will do what it takes to win; beliefs anyone can adopt to have better results in their personal or professional life.

If you adopt the following beliefs, you will win much more often.

Failure does Not Exist

Just because I crashed the last five times on the luge track does not mean I'll crash the next time. Every time I come down that track, I am a better racer because I am more experienced than on the previous run. That is, if I learn something from my mistake, and then apply the knowledge on that next run.

When Thomas Edison was trying to find the right filament to make the light bulb work, a reporter asked him how it felt to have failed thousands of times. Edison said he hadn't failed. He said that he had just discovered thousands of materials that didn't work. Edison wasn't being a smart-aleck. He was protecting his positive attitude by refusing to believe he had failed.

High achievers believe that they are destined to accomplish great things in their lifetimes. They believe that the challenges they experience are there to teach them a lesson they need to learn in order to complete their "mission" in life. They believe there is no such thing as failure. They either get the desired outcome or else they learn something that will help them win in the future. No matter what the result, they win. The past does not equal the future. By thinking this way, discouragement can't get a foothold in their mind.

If It Is To Be It Is Up To Me

Every single one of the people in the biographies I read had to overcome major challenges on the road to success. Struggling through those challenges is what made them great. A piece of coal has to experience a huge amount of heat and pressure in order to become a diamond. We are no different. Every time we face a challenge we have a choice to make. Will we get bitter or better? Decide to get better. Face the challenge. It's there to make you stronger. You will need that strength further up the road when you'll be facing even bigger challenges.

Don't ever make excuses. Whenever you make an excuse, you are giving up control. If you do make an excuse for not pursuing your dream, make sure it's a good one, because you'll have to live with it for the rest of

Take a chance. You'll never know what you were missing in life until you dare to pursue your dream.

your life. Don't rationalize. Rationalizing is telling yourself "rational lies."

Believe that you are in charge of your life. You are totally responsible. You create your results. You are in control of your life. You have the power to change your circumstances.

Commit to Win

Some people are interested in reaching their dreams and others are committed to reaching their dreams. The key to success in life is going from being interested to being committed. Once you are committed you will produce results. At the point of commitment, you mentally "burn all the bridges" and you start doing whatever it takes to make it happen. That's when you become unstoppable.

On the road to the Olympics, many athletes much faster than me quit along the way. There are only two reasons they quit; they either didn't want it badly enough or they were not as committed.

Commitment is what makes success possible. If you commit to do whatever it takes (as long as it is moral, legal and ethical) to succeed, success will reveal its secrets to you. There are four different levels of commitment; I'll try, I'll do my best, I'll do whatever it takes, and It's a done deal.

"I'll try" is completely worthless. Whenever someone tells you they are going to try to do something, don't count on anything ever happening. People say "I'll try" when they are afraid to say "I won't." "I'll try" is the battle cry of wimps. Whenever you say "I'll try," you have just guaranteed failure. Because saying "I'll try" is in effect saying, "If there are any obstacles, I'll have a way out and I'll be able to justify quitting."

"I'll do my best" is not much better than "I'll try." People that say "I'll do my best" are looking for a way out. When they say they'll do their best, they're leaving a huge door open for excuses and justifications later. Remember when you asked your buddies to help you move to your first apartment? I know for sure that none of the ones who said "I'll try to be there" or "I'll do my best to be there," showed up.

Winners say, "I'll do whatever it takes." If you tell

someone you'll do whatever it takes, you have to produce or else you'll lose face. Finally, the strongest level of commitment is when you say, "It's a done deal." When you say "It's a done deal," even losing face is not an option. When I was training for the Olympics I would not dare tell my coach I was going to try to do something. It was always, "It's a done deal."

We walked the track with the coach. We made a game plan about the best way to drive the track. We visualized and mentally rehearsed the ideal run, but sooner or later, we had to commit. Sooner or later, we had to hop on the sled and slide down the mountain. We had to take those runs knowing that even with all the preparation, the first few times down that track were going to be pretty brutal. Was it scary? Sure, it was scary. But you have to pay the price if you want to enjoy the prize. You have to commit to do things that are beyond your current abilities. That's the only way to grow. That's how you get better and stronger. So attack your fears head on. Otherwise, you will be their servant for the rest of your life.

Take a chance. Act on faith. Put yourself in a position where you have to stretch and fight for something. It brings out the best in you. It is good for your soul.

"The choice is yours. You hold the tiller. You can steer the course you choose in the direction of where you want to be – today, tomorrow, or in a distant time to come."

- W. Clement Stone

How to Succeed When Conditions Change

What do you say to yourself when market conditions, or your work or home conditions change? Do you see change as a good thing or as a bad thing?

One of my old success audio programs says, "Success is about change – not challenge." I was never sure about what that meant until one day, when I was playing racquetball with my good friend Todd Guest.

Todd is Chief Accounting Officer of an energy company based in Houston. Todd was killing me on the racquetball court. Todd has this powerful slam serve that I just could not return. He was scoring all these easy points and he beat me the first three games straight.

I started to feel frustrated; then sorry for myself; and finally, mad. My anger caused me to completely change my game. I unconsciously transformed my style from a finesse game to a speed and power game. I won the fourth game handily and Todd said "Looks like you made an adjustment and it worked."

We took a short break to get some water and started talking about success, change, and how it is so important to make an adjustment when you are not getting the desired results. Todd used his son as an example.

Todd's oldest son Kyle is a very good baseball player. Kyle's been playing on All Star baseball teams for as long as I can remember. We were talking about Kyle's success in baseball and Todd pointed out how successful baseball hitters constantly adjust to different pitchers and different circumstances. The same is true in any sport. Watch any tennis match and notice how one player wins the first set, then the other player adjusts and takes the second and so on.

The same is true in luge. You need to be ready to adjust to changing weather conditions and to changes in track conditions. The quicker you adjust, the better off you are.

Conditions change constantly. At work, in the marketplace, at home, life, in general, you have two choices. You can get bitter or you can suck it up, make an adjustment, and get better. Success is about change, not challenge. Those who adjust first, usually overcome the obstacle, they get ahead of the competition and are more likely to win.

Do you accept change? If you do, you need to stop accepting it. Accepting change is putting up with change. If you are only accepting change, you still have a bad attitude and you'll never be your best if your attitude is negative.

You need to start embracing change. You need to welcome change. Because changing conditions make you better at whatever you do. Changing conditions give you an opportunity to shine because, whenever there is change, whoever adapts first, wins. Change keeps the game interesting. Start praying for change. It gives you a chance to shine.

I'd like to tell you that I went on to win the fifth racquetball game, but Todd adjusted to my power game and won the last game. Todd, I'll get you next time!

Insanity: Doing the same thing and expecting different results. To get better results you must constantly adjust.

"It is not because things are difficult that we do not dare, it is because we do not dare that they are difficult."

-Seneca

How to Manage and Minimize Risk

We stood in the plaza for hours, trying to stay warm in spite of the chilly Pyrenees Mountain morning. Gathered with us were about 3,000 people of all ages from across the globe who, like us, were drawn to Pamplona by the mystique of running with the bulls.

You could feel the tension rise with each tick of the clock, drawing us nearer to 8:00 AM and the much anticipated release of six bulls and several steers into the cobblestoned streets of Pamplona. Only 15 to 20 feet wide, the half-mile course offered no escape route. However, since bulls can run much faster than people, it did promise the certainty that, in time, everyone would be overtaken by the bulls.

The wait was longer than the Bull Run itself, which only takes about 3 to 4 minutes—albeit, the most dangerous and exhilarating three minutes of your life.

There are always injuries. In fact, there are so many injuries that emergency medical crews and ambulances are stationed every 50 yards along the course. It was a given that someone would be hurt today. Occasionally, someone loses their life. Since 1910, 15 people have died running with the bulls. In 1995, a 22 year old American was gored to death less than 30 seconds after the beginning of the run. His first.

What drives people to risk their lives by running with the bulls? Some say you feel most alive when you are near

Running with the bulls in Pamplona, Spain

death. Others run for the challenge. Personally, I just think it's fun, exciting, and exhilarating.

Before going to Pamplona, I prepared by taking the same approach I take with everything. I sought knowledge from the experts. I read three books about Pamplona - each several times. I even contacted one of the authors, a man who's been running for 30 years, to pick his brain. Then, I spent many hours watching videos of the Bull Run to study the paths different runners took as they ran.

At first, the videos looked to me like nothing more than a horde of people running for their lives. After watching the videos over and over, though, I started to see well-defined patterns. All of a sudden, the things I had read about in the books started to make sense. I realized that there is a right way and a wrong way to run with the bulls.

I did my homework and that made all the difference.

What did I learn from all my studies? They gave me a handful of insights that drastically reduced my risk and turned a potentially deadly adventure into a science - or what became to me a strategic challenge.

Just like in business and in life, you find two types of people in the Bull Run. There are the amateurs who show up unprepared, wing it, and often get hurt. On the other hand, there are the professionals - experts who are armed with knowledge and skill and rarely get hurt.

In the Bull Run, 95% of the people are amateurs. The remaining 5% are the pros - the experts - the winners. Just like it is in business. Just like it is in life.

What did I learn from my research? I learned simple things that made a huge difference in my Pamplona experience.

First and most importantly, make sure to run sober and watch out for the drunks. There were lots of them out there. The drunks are more dangerous and more unpredictable than the bulls. The drunks trip, fall, and cause human pileups that you have to hurdle as you run down the street.

Secondly, if you fall, cover your head and stay down. The bulls will jump over you. If you get up, you become a big target and you could easily get hurt.

Third, tie your sash in a slip knot. Everyone in Pamplona dresses the same during the Fiesta - white shirt, white pants, red bandana around the neck, and a red sash around the waist. If you tie your sash in a double knot (like 95% of the amateurs did) and a bull's horn hooks your sash, the bull will drag you along the streets, your head bouncing off the cobblestones the whole way. Any tourist guide will tell you that this is not the best way to spend your time in Spain.

In life and in business, simple things can make a huge difference.

Finally, where do you run?

The half-mile course has five sections. Most of the deaths which have occurred were at the beginning and at the end. Most injuries and gorings occur at a sharp right hand curve in the middle of the course. Stay away from those three areas

At the Pamplona Bullring after the bull run.

unless you've been running for many years.

The whole time you are running you are deep in a narrow canyon made up of 10-story buildings on either side of the narrow streets. You are in the shade the whole time except right before you enter "Dead Man's Curve," or "La Curva" as it is known in Pamplona. Right before "La Curva," you are blinded by the early morning sun. The bulls are blinded, as well, and they slip on the moist cobblestones and slam into the retaining wall at the far side of the curve. Many injuries occur here when the runners get pinned by the falling bulls.

The experts suggest to begin the run about 50 yards past "La Curva" on the right side of the street. Why? Because the bulls tend to run on the left side of the street after passing "La Curva." By starting the run from the right side, you have a chance to gradually approach the bulls as you run down the long straightaway past the curve.

The top runners position themselves in the middle of the street and try to run right in front of the bulls' horns for as long as they can before they are overtaken. I was happy to run beside the bulls. Close, but not too close. I was actually running "from the bulls," not "with the bulls."

There is a bull run every morning for the eight days of the Fiesta. I was there for three days. I watched the first day and ran the second and the third. I'm definitely a beginner at this. Like everything else, practice makes perfect. I think it would take at least two to three years of running all eight days just to learn the basics. And then it would take a lifetime to master the basics.

So, what does all of this have to so with success? Everything. Whenever you are about to try anything new, something that looks too hard and too risky to be worthwhile, do what high achievers everywhere do. Don't try to figure it out on your own. You don't know what you don't know, and what you don't know can hurt you.

Rather, find the experts. Do your due diligence and minimize risk by learning from the best. Then, give yourself a couple of years to learn the basic skills by taking consistent and persistent action. By doing that, in time you will become the expert others turn to for advice. By pursuing excellence in everything you do, you will make your life a masterpiece.

"Expect trouble as an inevitable part of life and when it comes, hold your head high, look it squarely in the eye and say, 'I will be bigger than you. You cannot defeat me.'"

-Ann Landers

How to Develop the Courage to Succeed

No matter what your dream is, to make it a reality, you will have to have the courage to act in spite of your fears. High achievement requires courage, self-confidence, boldness, and the willingness to go for your goals with no guarantee of success. With courage you can do anything in life. Without it, none of the other qualities will help you.

We all admire people who have overcome great challenges on the way to success; people who have a dream, and have the courage to commit fully to it. Winners have that rare attitude of not worrying about the possibility of failure. They go for it and commit 100% to winning no matter what. Their attitude is, "It's my dream and I'm going for it. That's it period."

When you move boldly towards you goals, when you make the decision to do whatever it takes, magic happens. All of a sudden, unseen forces will come to your aid. The bolder and more committed you are, the more your subconscious will work for you. You will unconsciously start to attract the people and resources you need to achieve your goal. All of a sudden, you will draw energy to making your dream a reality.

People will start saying you are lucky. Winners know there is no such thing as luck. All that is really happening is that now, you have become driven. You are becoming known for your goal. Everybody can see it. Your every action is broadcasting to the world where you are headed, and all of a sudden, anyone who might be interested in helping you, can see you are serious.

When you are focused on your goal, your mind starts acting like a guided missile. It becomes tuned to anything that might help you achieve your goal. This is not any different than when you buy a new car and all of a sudden you notice how many other people are driving the same model car.

When you put all of your energy into one goal, you tap into huge resources. That single decision changes everything. All of the stress and worry disappears.

> *Fortune favors the brave. Boldness has magic in it.*

Your mental attitude changes completely. You are now the hunter. The dream has become the prey that will eventually succumb to you.

When you make the decision to commit 100%, the winner inside you comes out. The champion inside you comes out. The real you comes out. You just have to have the courage to face your fears.

Your fears are a smokescreen. They are like ghosts that keep you from being the real you. Your best you. It's OK to be afraid. Everyone is afraid. If everyone is afraid, what's the difference between a brave person and a coward? The brave person acts in spite of his fears. The coward allows his fears to overwhelm him and control his thoughts, feelings and behaviors.

Can courage be developed? Absolutely. Aristotle said, "You become what you repeatedly do." Do you realize the implications of that statement? It means we are not doomed to being the way we currently are. You can change. You can grow. You can be a different person three months from now. In case you haven't figured it out, that excites me. You see, if that is true, and it is, now you know that it is within you to grow into the kind of person that can make your dreams come true. And you'd better constantly change and grow. Because in life you don't get what you want. You get what you become because you attract success by the person you become.

The way to develop courage is by practicing courage in every situation where courage is required. How do you do that? By making a single quality decision. You come to the realization that whenever you are afraid to do something, you are simply being tested. You make a decision that from now on you will win over your fear. Remember; if you do what you fear, the fear will disappear. If you don't do what you fear, the fear will control your life.

Make a game out of conquering your fears. You can get started with small things. For example, if you usually wait to see what everyone else is having when you're ordering in a restaurant, next time, decide to be the first to order. When you do that, you will have experienced

Winners develop the courage to get started and the courage to endure.

a small personal victory. You just won over that fear. Next time you are talking to somebody and you want to ask a question but you are afraid of looking stupid, ask anyways. Guess what? You've just won another personal victory. Score: Fears – 0, Courage –2.

You need to win many personal victories before you will win a public victory. Michael Johnson, the 200 meter and 400 meter Olympic Gold medalist, says in his biography, "I did not miss a scheduled workout in 10 years." He had thousands of private victories before experiencing his public victory.

By becoming conscious of your fears and making a game out of conquering them, before long you will begin

117

to understand in your heart that fears are just smokescreens. And by playing that game all the time, you are becoming more courageous every day.

There are two parts of courage that lead to success. The first part is the willingness to begin, to act in faith, to step out boldly in the direction of your goals with no guarantee of success. The second part of courage is the willingness to endure, to persist, to refuse to give up, and to keep on working harder than anyone else.

Most people talk themselves out of even going for their dream. And most of the ones who make the attempt quit as soon as the going gets tough. It's so sad. Because everyone has the ability to make their dreams come true. It's sad that so few people have the willingness to do what it takes.

That's why as a boy I admired the Olympians. That's why we root for the underdog. That's why we love movies like Rocky and Rudy. That's why we admire people like speed skater Dan Jansen. Because all of us have felt like the underdog at one time or another. Because seeing the underdog win gives us hope that we can win too.

Once you get started on the road to making your dreams a reality, you must make the decision to never quit. The decision to never give up gives you a huge advantage. The person who is most determined usually wins. A study on goals and perseverance found that 95% of the goals that people set are ultimately achieved, as long as the person didn't give up.

Ninety five percent. That's almost a guarantee. A guarantee that if you refuse to quit you will eventually win. The main reason people fail is not because of lack of ability or opportunities. They fail because they lack the inner strength to persist in the face of obstacles and difficulties. That's why trying something almost always leads to failure. By definition, trying something means you will quit if you are not successful.

118

Don't worry about failing. Failing is how you learn. You can fail over and over again, but all it takes is one big success to wipe out all your previous failures. Just like Dan Jansen in the Lillehammer Olympics. The only time you can't afford to fail is the last time you try.

You need to be bold. Once you have made the decision to never quit, it's easy to be bold. Remember, if you don't quit you're almost guaranteed to succeed. So just assume that success is inevitable. It's only a matter of time. Act as if your ultimate success is guaranteed. No matter how bad it is or how bad it gets, learn from your failures and keep moving on.

Your goal should be to reach the point where you believe in yourself so much that nothing can stop you or hold you back for very long. You want to become unstoppable. This is where persistence is so important. The more you persist, the more you will believe in yourself. And the more you believe in yourself, the more you persist. Your persistence is a measure of how much you believe in yourself and how much you believe in your ability to succeed.

> **Courage is acting in spite of your fears.**

If you act as if you are guaranteed to succeed, your belief will grow. Why? Because emotion follows motion. What you do determines how we will feel. Act in spite of your fears and commit to not quit, and I'll promise you that the winner inside you will burst forth to propel you to victory.

When you develop your courage and perseverance, you will experience life in ways you never thought were possible. The more you practice courage and perseverance, the more confident you will become. Don't quit. Refuse to quit and you will succeed. Dan Jansen refused to quit and look at what happened...

Dan Jansen was supposed to win gold in the Sarajevo

1984 Olympics. He didn't. Disappointed, he knew he should bring home a medal in the 1988 Calgary games. But only moments before the start of the race he was told his sister, Jane had died of leukemia. With this weighing on his mind, he raced poorly and walked home empty handed. Dan had another chance in Nagano 1992, but his hopes were crushed again when he slipped on the ice. The 1994 Lillehammer would be his last chance.

With the world holding its breath as he raced in the 500 meters, he fell again to the horror of the crowd, and finished eighth. With only one race left in his career, the 1000, Dan Jansen was racing for his life. Incredibly he slipped on the last turn, but didn't fall. As he raced past the finish line, he read the official time. A new world record. At long last Dan Jansen's perseverance paid off. Finally he had won the Olympic Gold Medal. On his victory lap, he carried his baby daughter on his shoulders. Her name is Jane, after Dan's sister.

> *Do the things you fear, or else fear will control your life.*

Dan's story is so inspirational. It makes us feel like we can't fail. It teaches us lessons in courage and perseverance. It has been said, "The Honor should not go to those who have not fallen; rather, all Honor should go to those who fall and rise again." That's why we love Rocky, and Rudy, and the Olympics.

Have the courage to go after your dream. Give it all you've got. Have the courage to get started and have the courage to never quit. I guarantee you, when you do, your life will become great.

*"It is not the mountain
we conquer but ourselves."*

- Sir Edmund Hillary

*"I am the master of my fate.
I am the Captain of my soul."*

- William Henley

The Power to Choose

In his book "Roots," Alex Haley tells about something unexpected that happened right after slavery was abolished. The newly freed slaves did not know how to be free. All their lives they had had others make their decisions for them, consequently, they had never learned how to make their own choices. You could say their "choice-making muscles" needed developing. Some of the slaves actually stayed with their masters and worked for them for the rest of their lives as free men.

In the movie "The Shawshank Redemption," when Brooks, the prison librarian, who's been an inmate for 50 years, is set free, he does not know how to be a free man. He does not know how to use his power to choose. All his life he has been told what to do. For Brooks, life as a free man is so overwhelming, that he ends up committing suicide.

Most people's "choice-making muscles" could use a little strengthening. After all, when we are young, our parents and our teachers tell us what to do. Then we get a job and our boss tells us what to do. It seems like there's always somebody telling us what to do.

We start drifting through life instead of designing our future. We start existing instead of living. And we end up using a fraction of our gifts. We forget that we have the power to choose who we want to be, what we want to accomplish, where we want to live, etc. We stop taking responsibility for our results, and start living as a victim, instead of as a victor.

You and I have the power to choose what we do with our lives. You are where you are because of the choices you've made. If you don't like where you are, you need to start making different choices. I've been in sales all my life. Whenever I've ever had a slow sales month, I could always trace it to lack of activity a few months back. Likewise, whenever my pants start feeling tight around the waist, I can always trace it to having been overeating recently. It's not rocket science.

My dad always told me, "It's not what happens to you, it's how you handle it." He also said to me, "You have the power to choose your destiny." It wasn't until I started acting like I believed those things that my life started getting interesting.

I have a little secret for you. There is a magical moment between your circumstances and your results. That moment is called CHOICE. When something happens to you, when circumstances happen to you, when things that seem unfair happen to you, don't whine and complain. The instant you start blaming your circumstances is the instant you become a victim. Once you do that, you are relinquishing control and then you can kiss your future goodbye. Remember, you can choose your response to those circumstances. Make a wise choice, handle it properly, and watch your results improve tremendously.

Sometimes the choice you need to make is to learn a new skill or improve something about your life. Because for things to change in your life, you've got to change. For things to get better, you have to get better. What kind of life do you want? The good news is that you have the power to create it.

Don't wish things were easier; wish you were better. Don't wish for less problems; wish for more skills. Don't wish for less challenges; wish for more wisdom.

Once you stop making excuses and start taking

responsibility for your results, your life will start getting really exciting. It did for me.

"Whatever you believe you can do, begin it. Action has magic, power, and grace to it."

- Goethe

How to Create Extraordinary Results

Leaders in every field agree that there is a shortage of people who get things done; people who get results. That is great news. It's an opportunity for all of us. What that means is that, if you want to move up in your field, all you have to do is to start getting results. So how do you do that? By becoming a person of action. Massive action.

Having good ideas is not enough. Even having great ideas is not enough. Ideas are a dime a dozen. However, people that implement ideas are priceless. Everything that exists in this world is the product of an idea that was acted upon. Even the chair you're sitting on was the product of an idea which was acted upon.

Successful people are active. They get things done. They don't waste any time. They have an urgency about them. Passive people are not successful. Passive people procrastinate. Put things off. They wait for everything to be perfect before acting.

I've got news for you: conditions have never been or never will be perfect. What if Eisenhower had waited until conditions were perfect to invade Normandy? What if Kennedy had waited until conditions were perfect before deciding to put a man on the moon? What if Columbus had waited for conditions were perfect before setting out on his voyage?

If I had waited until conditions were perfect, I never would have tried out for my college soccer team, I never would have taken up the sport of luge, I never would have trained for the Olympics, I never would have asked my wife on our first date, I never would have had a daughter or a son, and I never would have started my own business. Consequently, if I had waited until conditions were perfect, I would have missed out on the most exciting parts of my life.

Commitment creates opportunity. Stop talking and start doing. Think less and act more.

When you are about to take a family vacation you probably don't wait until all the lights are green. You get started and you handle the red lights as you come across them. Start using that approach with everything else. Get started, and handle the challenges as they come along.

Do something. Get started. Move. Generate some momentum. If you don't, you'll regret it and you will be filled with stress. Stress comes from not doing what you know you should be doing.

Once you get started, once you are in motion, your mind starts focusing on how to get the job done. As soon as you get in motion, you move ahead of the competition. All those poor souls who are still "thinking about it," miss the opportunities.

Action produces confidence. Inaction strengthens fear. Every time you take a risk, you expand your comfort zone. Just think about when you were a kid on the high dive in your neighborhood pool. The longer you waited to dive, the worse the fear got. But once you decided to dive, the fear was gone, and you spent the rest of the afternoon diving. Taking action made it fun. Taking action made it exhilarating.

You know what you need to do. Do it now. Get going.

128

Get started. Become an action fanatic. And act boldly – make a decision and never look back. You'll be glad you did.

If you're not willing to take action, do us all a favor and stop talking about it!

"You are the captain of the ship called you. You're setting the course, the speed, and you're out there on the bridge, steering."

- Carl Frederick

PART THREE

Stories that Will Help You Win

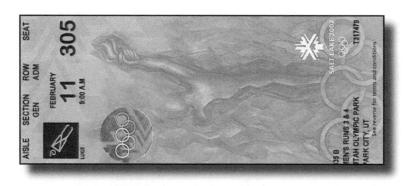

2002 Salt Lake City Olympic Luge Ticket

"A man owes very little to what he is born with – a man is what he makes of himself."

- Alexander Graham Bell

How to Design
Your Own Life

We each have the responsibility to design our lives. The power to fulfill our dreams is within each of us. The day you take complete responsibility for yourself, the day you stop making excuses, is the day you start moving to the top.

Success is up to you. Success will not fall on your lap. You have to go out and get it. You have to fight for it. Some people use every circumstance as an excuse to justify why they are not getting the results they want. Winners refuse to make excuses. No matter how dire their circumstances are, they simply focus on the goal and keep on keeping on.

My brother Marcelo is a real winner. The story of what he had to overcome to make it to the Olympics is truly amazing.

I competed in the 1988 Calgary and in the 1992 Albertville Winter Olympics. In 1992, I met my wife Cheryl, and she totally derailed me. All of a sudden I had a new dream. So, I broke up with my sled and I started dating Cheryl. I retired from the luge and did not slide for six years.

Five years before the 2002 Salt Lake City Olympics, Coach called me on the phone.

Coach said, "Ruben, the sport of luge needs Argentina again."

I told him, "Forget it Coach, I'm done with luge. I have a family and I've already done the Olympic thing."

Coach is a winner. He didn't take no for an answer. He

kept calling.

"Ruben, Salt Lake will be a great Olympic Games. The U.S. has the best Olympic Spirit. You still have five years to train. You must come back. You'll regret it if you don't."

"No thanks Coach."

But he was planting a seed. Now he had me thinking about it.

Coach called again.

"Okay, Ruben, here's the deal. I'm putting together a two week luge training camp in Calgary. You get yourself to Calgary and I'll take care of your room, your board, and all your track fees for two weeks. After two weeks, you tell me if you want to come back, no questions asked."

At that point I knew Coach was serious. Heck, in all the years I'd known him, Coach had never even bought me a drink and here he was offering to pay for thousands of dollars worth of training.

So I countered, "All right Coach, here's the deal. I have a brother who has seen me go to two Olympics and I've seen the look in his eyes. If your deal goes for him too, I'll go. After all, we still have five years before the Salt Lake City Olympics. Who knows? Maybe he can make it."

Coach asked, "How old is he?"

"Thirty years old."

"Thirty years old???!!! Forget it."

I told him, "Coach, you've got to see this guy. He's an awesome athlete. He can do it!"

Marcelo wasn't a great athlete. He was an architect. He was the artsy kind of guy. I don't think he had ever broken into a voluntary sweat before. But Marcelo was mentally tough as nails. That's what made me think he could do it.

Coach answered, "Okay. Bring him along." And he hung up on me.

After the phone call, I went over to Marcelo, who did not have any idea that I was negotiating for him. I said,

"Marcelo, look, here's the deal: worst case scenario, you've got a free two week vacation. Best case scenario: you could become an Olympian. You've got nothing to lose."

Marcelo said, "Sounds good to me."

We went to Calgary. After the first day of sliding, I knew I was back. Meanwhile, Marcelo caught the Olympic Dream. As soon as we got back home, he started working out like a fiend and got himself into terrific shape. Marcelo made a decision to pursue the dream; to take the journey; to face the struggle with no guarantees of success.

The day you take complete responsibility for yourself, the day you stop making any excuses, is the day you start moving to the top.

Every boss I've ever worked for supported my quest for the Olympics by allowing me to take off a few months a year to train. It was time off without pay, but at least I knew I had a job when I came back. They could see that the fact that I was using my job in the pursuit of my dream, inspired the rest of their employees to work harder, because now they saw how they could use their jobs as a vehicle for their dreams.

Marcelo's boss didn't see it that way. Marcelo had been working for another architect for five years. As soon as Marcelo's boss realized how serious he was about pursuing his Olympic quest, he old Marcelo, "You have to make a choice: either work for me or train for the Olympics."

At that point, most people would have quit on their dream and would have spent the rest of their lives regretting it. Marcelo went for the dream and quit his job. He was committed to his dream and he was not about to let anybody steal it from him.

Then Marcelo did something really smart. Over the years,

he had developed strong relationships with contractors in the Houston area. So rather than getting another job and risking having another unsupportive boss, Marcelo started his very own architectural firm, GonzalezArchitects.com.

His contractor friends sent him a lot of business and from day one Marcelo had a steady stream of clients. He worked from his home for the first four years and, later on, he moved his firm to an office building in one of the most prestigious areas of Houston.

There is opportunity in every challenge.

That's what winners do. They always look ahead to where they want to be and they work hard to position themselves to be in a place of power when opportunity strikes.

Losers don't plan ahead. They hope their dreams will drop on their lap. Later, when their plans don't work, they spend the rest of their lives whining about how unlucky they were.

Marcelo learned the luge and started competing internationally. In order to compete in the Olympics, he had to get good enough to crack into the top fifty in the world.

In November of 2001, just three months before the Olympics, we were racing in a world cup race in Calgary. I had just finished my final run and was at the bottom of the track with all the other athletes who had finished the race. We were all standing by a TV monitor watching the remaining racers' runs.

Marcelo came barreling down the track and, right before entering the finish curve, his sled slammed into the straightaway wall. The impact sent him flying straight up to "the woods," a small retaining wall that creates a lip over the curves. The woods are there to prevent the lugers from flying off the track. However, when you hit the woods, it's very easy to break a knee.

Marcelo hit the woods very hard. He went so much higher than the normal line sleds take, that his sled hit a patch of concrete up at the top of the curve. When his steel runners hit the concrete, he shot sparks six feet long. It looked like an explosion behind him.

Well, what goes up must come down. Marcelo fell about twenty feet, hit the bottom of the track, bounced back up, smashed into the woods again, and came to a stop at the end of the curve. His crash caused him to decelerate from seventy miles per hour to zero in less than two seconds.

It was a very rough crash. We are all used to seeing crashes, however, when Marcelo crashed, there was a collective gasp from all the athletes. We all figured he'd probably broken both his legs and totaled his sled.

Incredibly, after a couple of minutes, Marcelo climbed out of the track and limped out on his own. For the rest of the season, he limped a bit when he walked. But he didn't complain once, he iced his knee, which was swollen to the size of a melon.

Marcelo kept sliding and endured a couple of other crashes in the remaining season, all which must have hurt his knee even more. It seems that whenever you get injured in the luge, all you ever do is to keep re-injuring the injury. But Marcelo never complained.

That's just Marcelo's style. He's like the tortoise in "The Tortoise and the Hare." He just keeps on moving on. I'm sure glad he's wired that way because I had to room with him all season. I'd rather wrap myself in a blanket and sleep in the hallway than to have to room with a negative person.

Back when I played college soccer, a couple of guys in the team were chronic complainers. Coach did something very smart. He always made them room together so their bad attitude would not infect the rest of the team. After a while they both ended up quitting. Good riddance.

I'm sure you have a couple of whiners in your office, too.

They are always complaining about one thing or another and nobody ever wants to be around them. Everyone wishes they would just quit.

Marcelo didn't whine. He kept racing despite his injuries. He kept accumulating those World Cup points. He kept his focus on breaking into the top fifty.

Two races before the Olympics, I broke into the top fifty. I was pretty beat up from the long season, so I decided to skip the last race. At that point, it looked like I was going to the Olympics and Marcelo was staying home. It didn't look like he could make up the difference. Then, on the last race of the season, Marcelo had a great result and ended up ranked forty-ninth in the world. The thirty six year-old architect was going to the Olympics.

On February 8th, 2002, Marcelo and I made Olympic history. We became the first set of brothers to ever compete against each other in the Olympic luge. Dreams do come true if you believe and if you take massive action.

Marcelo and I had promised each other that after the race we would go take some ski lessons. You see, even though the luge tracks are next to some of the best skiing in the world, we were always afraid of hurting ourselves skiing and ruining a luge season. As a result, we had never even learned how to ski. I was probably the only three-time Winter Olympian in the world who had never even skied.

The day after our race, we took some ski lessons and skied all afternoon. On the way back to the Olympic Village, Marcelo said his knee was really hurting so he would get it checked out. That evening, he got an MRI and an x-ray done. The result? Marcelo had a broken kneecap.

We kept the x-rays of Marcelo's knee because it was incredible. The fracture looks just like one of those "no smoking" signs: a circle with a line crossed through it.

The doctors could not believe that Marcelo could ski with a broken knee. They said he should have had trouble

138

Marcelo and I in Sigulda, Latvia.

walking. When Marcelo told the physicians that he had broken the kneecap three months before and had qualified for the Olympics, it blew them away.

Vince Lombardi said, "The good Lord gave you a body that can stand most everything. It's your mind you have to convince." Don't fall into the trap of using your health as an excuse for not pursuing your dream.

Marcelo took responsibility for himself. He didn't use his circumstances as an excuse. He focused on what he had to do and by doing so, he not only made his Olympic Dream come true, but he helped create Olympic history.

What about you? Will you just hope your dreams come true or will you make a decision to pursue your dreams? Go for it. Doing so will change your life.

Marcelo and I at Salt Lake City Opening Ceremonies

If it is to be it is up to you. Nobody can succeed for you. You have to make it happen. There is no one to stop you but yourself. Make it happen.

"There are always opportunities through which people can profit handsomely if they will only recognize and seize them."

- J. Paul Getty

How to Make
Your Own Luck

Opportunity is everywhere. You have to keep your eyes open and focus on finding it. Once you spot an opportunity, if you decide you are willing to do whatever it takes, it's only a matter of time before you get what you want.

In November 1987, we had just arrived at the luge track in St. Moritz, Switzerland. We were about to begin training and qualifying for the World Cup Race that weekend. The International Luge World Cup Circuit is like a traveling circus. Every week, you see the same group of athletes at a different track. As I mentioned earlier, we typically travel on Mondays; train and qualify, Tuesday through Friday; race on the weekends; then travel to the next track.

As soon as we got to the St. Moritz track, I noticed something was different. There were only three sleds signed up in the doubles competition. Doubles luge is a wild sport consisting of two athletes lying on the same sled. They both steer, but only the top man can see. The top man gives body signals to the bottom man to tell him when to steer. It takes years to develop the trust, communication skills, and teamwork required to do well in doubles. I'd never done it. I'm a singles luge racer. But only three sleds. What an opportunity!

I ran to my best luge buddy, Pablo Garcia of Spain, and excitedly told him, "This is our chance. We'll never have another opportunity like this! We have to find a doubles sled and race. If one of those other three sleds crashes, we'll have a World Cup Medal."

Pablo's no dummy. He saw the opportunity right away. We convinced Coach to let us race. We told him the opportunity was too good to pass up. The opportunity was worth the risk of injury. It took a while to convince Coach, but finally he gave in, saying, "If you can find a doubles sled in St. Moritz, you can race."

Finding a doubles sled in St. Moritz was going to be a real challenge. Even though they have a track, St. Moritz is not a big luge town. They love Bobsled and Skeleton (head-first luge), but hardly anyone in St. Moritz does the luge. That didn't matter to us. We were determined to do whatever it took to make it happen. I spent two days knocking on doors all around the town asking the locals if they had a doubles sled we could borrow.

Take a leap of faith. Jump and the net will appear.

I was cold-calling in a foreign country – in a town that does not like lugers. They speak German in St. Moritz. I don't. But it didn't matter. When you want something badly enough, the facts don't count. You just do it. I knocked on doors, regurgitated a German phrase I had memorized – "Haben zie ein doppelsitzer rennrodeln schlitten fur die weltcup renn?" and hoped they nodded.

Eventually, I found a man who had a twenty-year-old rusted out sled in his shed. He agreed to let us borrow it. We spent the next two days getting that antique sled race-ready.

On race day, everyone came out to see Pablo and I kill ourselves trying to do doubles. We almost did. We were on the verge of crashing the whole way down. But we finished the race, placed fourth, and actually received a World Cup Medal (we'd never even seen a 4th place medal before, they

Pablo Garcia and I in Albertville, France

usually only award medals to the top three finishers), got our pictures in the paper, and best of all, we earned so many World Cup Points for coming in fourth, that by season's end, we had a world ranking of 14th in the doubles!

The following week, the word that Pablo and I had taken fourth in the World Cup spread like wildfire in the luge circuit. Some of the athletes who had not shown up in St. Moritz heard about what we had done, but passed off our victory saying, "we were lucky." Pablo and I explained to them that "luck had nothing to do with it." We simply had seen an opportunity, and made a decision to do whatever it took to win, and in the end, won. We made our own luck.

I guarantee you that if you will develop that attitude – the attitude that you will go for it and give it your all, your life will be a lot more fun. People will be amazed at the things you accomplish. Jump and the net will appear. It really will.

145

"The credit belongs to the man who is actually in the arena; whose face is marred by dust and sweat and blood; who strives valiantly; who errs and comes short again and again; who knows the great enthusiasms, the great devotions, and spends himself in a worthy cause; who at best knows in the end the triumph of high achievement; and who at the worst, if he fails, at least fails while daring greatly."

- Theodore Roosevelt

How to Turn
Defeat into Victory

I'll never forget it. We were training for a week in Sarajevo, Yugoslavia, an ancient city in Eastern Europe. We had a couple of hours to kill so we visited the old city. The streets in Old Sarajevo are too narrow for vehicles. The air is filled with smoke because many people still burn wood for heat. And everywhere you look you see towering minarets, a constant reminder that you are now in Eurasia, far from home. Walking the cobbled streets of Old Sarajevo makes you feels like you have been transported back in time.

Imagine my surprise when I walked into a smoke-filled café for a hot cup of Turkish coffee and heard the TV blaring in English! Back then, nobody spoke English in Sarajevo. Everyone spoke Serbo-Croatian. The TV was tuned in to ESPN. I was hooked. That cold morning I saw a commercial that I'll never forget. You've probably seen it, too. This is how the commercial went...

"Over 3000 times I've been called upon by my company to perform and I did not do what I was expected to do. Twenty-six times the company has called on me for the day's final activities and I failed. Three hundred times I've been a part of my company's total failure. And I'm still considered to be the greatest basketball player that has ever lived. I'm Michael Jordan.

Three thousand times I've been called upon to shoot the

basketball at the basket and missed. Twenty six times my team has asked me to shoot the final shot in the game and I missed. I've been part of over 300 losses of the Chicago Bulls.

Next time the Bulls play and there are two to three seconds left in the game everyone knows who will be called to take the last shot. He is not afraid of losing. He is not afraid of defeat."

Wow! Michael Jordan's commercial came at a good time for me. At the time, the track in Sarajevo was the fastest in the world. We reached speeds of over ninety five miles per hour from the Men's Start. At that speed you feel like you're a cassette player stuck on fast forward and you can't find the stop button. I don't know about the other guys, but I felt fear on every run. I just got myself to act in spite of fear so I could make my dream come true.

Fear is a smokescreen. Act in spite of your fear and the fear will disappear.

And that's exactly what you need to do. Act in spite of your fears. Every time you do something you fear, you gain strength, confidence, courage, and faith. Every time. You must always stop and look fear in the face and do what you think you cannot do. How do you do that? Simple: by finding a dream big enough to overcome your fears; a dream that takes your breath away.

Any successful person will tell you the same thing. They'll tell you that they failed themselves to success. I have taken a couple of thousand luge runs since 1984. Out of all those runs, I remember only two runs that I was really proud of. Two luge runs that I nailed. I was proud of them but even that is relative. I'll bet my coach, who was a three-time World Champion, thought that even those two runs were nothing to brag about. But you know what? Those two

148

thousand "failures" got me to the Olympics four times. I failed my way to success. You could say I crashed my way to the top.

If your dream is big enough, you'll be able to go from one failure to another without losing enthusiasm. Before long, you'll look back and you'll see those failures for what they really were: success school. The failures you experience give you the education you need to begin to succeed. Once you start to succeed, the trick is to learn to go from one success to another without losing humility.

The Turkish coffee was a little strong, but I'm sure glad I walked into that Sarajevo coffee shop.

"It's all right to be Goliath, but always act like David."

- Phil Knight – Founder of Nike

How to Make a Difference in People's Lives

There are several definitions of character. One definition is how you act when no one is looking at you. Another definition of character is: how you treat people who could not possibly help you in any way.

How you treat people who cannot help you says a lot about you. Do you ignore them? Do you walk over them? Or do you encourage them and help them out?

What difference does it make? It makes a huge difference. Character is a big part of leadership because people are more likely follow and trust you if you are a person of character. They will want to develop long-term relationships with you. If you're in sales (and by the way, everyone is in sales), they will buy more often and buy more product from you. Your whole quality of life improves if you are a person of character.

The 2002 luge season was a tough one for me. All season long I was plagued with injuries that made it hard for me to get into any kind of good rhythm. My injuries made it hard for me to focus as much as I needed to and, consequently, my sliding was very sloppy.

I compensated by playing it safe. By taking less risks down the track and, as a result, I didn't crash once during the regular season. That sounds like a good thing, but, really, it's not. You see, by taking very safe lines down the track, my times were very slow. I needed to take more risks. Especially on training runs where you have an opportunity to try out different lines to find the best ones to use on race day.

With a couple of weeks left in the season, I bet Coach that if I made it through the season and through the Olympics without crashing, he needed to buy me a new speed-suit. That was a big mistake on my part. Instead of focusing on not crashing, I should have been focusing on getting better race times. As Coach agreed on the bet, he had one of those funny smiles that told me he knew something I didn't know.

Somehow, I made it through the regular season without any crashes. Now we're at the Salt Lake City Olympics. Ten runs to go: six training runs and the four Olympic runs.

The Sarajevo track is no longer open. It's in the middle of a mine field; a victim of the Bosnian War. In 2002, the Salt Lake Track was the fastest in the world. Top speeds of eighty five miles per hour. The track was in unbelievable condition for the Olympics. Luge tracks are bumpy. They look smooth on TV but when you're sliding, it feels like you're racing a pickup truck down a dirt road. You usually have a splitting headache after just one run, and, later, must face taking several more runs.

The Salt Lake Olympic track was different. Someone told me the track workers had actually smoothed the ice with acetylene torches. The ice felt like glass. I was taking my first training run and it did not even feel like the luge. The run felt like a different sport. I was thinking, "This feels so great... so smooth... so good... so..." Instead of focusing on how well prepared the ice was, I should have been focusing on making it down the track. Crash!!!!

Without any warning, I had the second worst crash of my career. I didn't even see it coming. It caught me completely off guard. For the first time in my luge career, I was completely disoriented. I remember seeing the sky

152

twice and hitting the bottom of the track twice. The whole time thinking, "Please, God, don't let me brake any bones. I'm racing in the Olympics in two days."

Thank goodness, I didn't break anything. But for the next two days, whenever I went to the bathroom, there was blood in my urine. It scared me to death but I didn't dare go see the doctors because they would surely have scratched me from the race.* After the race, the Doctor examined me and determined that I had bruised my kidneys. No big deal.

Unfortunately, my sled was a mess. The steel runners were gouged and scratched so badly that I didn't think I would not be able to fix them in time for the race. The medics picked me up and drove me back to the Men's Start House at the top of the mountain.

I walked into the start house holding my sled. My face must have been ashen because all the other athletes there looked at me and starting mumbling in different languages. Then, something incredible happened. Jonathan Edwards walked right up to me, took a look at my sled, and said, "Give me thirty minutes and a file and I'll have your steels looking like new."

I didn't even know Jonathan Edwards. Jonathan had competed for the U.S. Team in the 1994 Lillehammer Winter Olympics during the time I had temporarily "retired" from the luge. In Salt Lake City Jonathan was coaching the Bermuda Luge Team.

---

* I'm not suggesting that you should not to go to the doctor when you are hurt; heck, as an athlete, I regularly visit doctors, chiropractors, and physical therapists to keep myself in optimal condition. However, in this case, I'd worked too hard for too long to lose it all at the last minute. I felt the prize justified the risk.

Jonathan Edwards working on my sled.

Jonathan had nothing to gain from helping me. He helped me because he has a big heart; he's a person of character; a person who is genuinely interested in helping other people out. He's just a terrific guy. Jonathan got me out of a terrible situation. He just showed up out of nowhere. Kind of like a guardian Angel.

It's very unusual to find someone like that. You want to be around people like that. What if we all strived to be a little bit more like Jonathan? Would we have more influence over everyone we meet? Would the world be a better place?

Character counts. Big time.

"Your character is what you really are, while your reputation is what others think you are."

- Coach John Wooden

"Far better it is to dare great things, to win glorious triumphs, even though checkered by failure, than to rank with those poor spirits who neither enjoy much nor suffer much, because they live in the gray twilight that knows neither victory nor defeat."

- *Theodore Roosevelt*

How to Build a Dream Team

Three months before the Salt Lake City Olympics, I got a great phone call. The lady on the phone told me, "Ruben, you've been selected to carry the Olympic Torch." The Olympic Torch! For an athlete, that's almost as good as winning a medal; almost.

The Torch is lit up at Mt. Olympia in Greece, home of the ancient Olympics. Then it was flown to Atlanta. Over ten thousand people were going to carry the Torch across the United States.

However, only two hundred Olympic athletes were going to get to carry the Torch. When they selected me, I felt like I'd just won the lottery.

I asked her, "When's it coming through Houston?"

She said, "December fifth."

"December fifth? Why December fifth? On December fifth, I'm competing in a World Cup race in Europe. I'm still trying to qualify for Salt Lake!"

The whole time I'm thinking to myself, "There is always a way, there is always a way, I have to figure out a way."

Then I said, "Wait a minute. I'll be back in January. I can carry it in January. I'll go anywhere in January. I'll go to Alaska. I'll walk to Alaska. I'll do whatever it takes. Just let me carry the Torch!"

The lady must have been impressed with my passion

because she said, "Hang on a minute. Let me check..." (I guarantee you that if I had said, "Oh, O.K. I guess I can't carry the Torch then, too bad..." She would not have gone out of her way to check on other dates and consequently, I would not have gotten to become a Torchbearer).

She put me on hold for a couple of very long minutes, and then returned to the line.

"Can you carry it in Kansas City on January ninth?"

"Absolutely! I'll be there! It's a done deal!" (Notice I didn't say "I'll try." or "I'll do my best." If I had, that would have been the end of the story. In life, wishy-washy doesn't work. Committed and passionate works).

Then I walked across the street to my neighbor Tom's house. Tom is one of the most supportive people I know. He's a big cheerleader. No matter how badly I mess something up, Tom always finds something positive about it. Always.

Every weekend, while I was training for the Olympics, Tom would wait until I was mowing my front lawn and, without fail, he would park his huge van right in front of my house, roll down the window, and start yelling like a madman, "I believe in you, Ruben! I'm going to see you on TV! You know why? Because you WILL... BE... A... THREE... TIME... OLYMPIAN!!!" Then he would peel out leaving a cloud of smoke.

After he did that, I was so pumped up with energy that I mowed my lawn in five minutes! Sometimes, I ran across the street and mowed Tom's lawn! Maybe that's why he did it! But seriously, how can you fail when you surround yourself with people like Tom? You can't.

It's critical to your success to build a Dream Team of key people who will get you up when the going gets tough. How do you build a Dream Team? How do you find people like Tom?

Back when I was twenty-one and decided to train for the Olympics, I realized that there are two kinds of people in the

158

world: people are either on your team or they are not in your team. They are either on your Dream Team or they are not. People will either encourage you or cast doubt. If they doubt you can do it, they could steal your dream away.

You see, a dreamer will never be understood by a non-dreamer. If a dreamer takes a non-dreamer's advice, he'll just go home, he won't do anything with his life, and ultimately die of a broken heart.

Associating with negative people makes us think negatively. Close contact with petty individuals develops petty habits in us. On the other hand, companionship with "big idea" type of people raises the level of our thinking. Close contact with ambitious people causes us to become more ambitious. Here's a great rule of thumb: If you're the smartest, or the most motivated person in your group, its time to find a new group.

> *Fly with eagles, you'll start to think, feel and act like an eagle.*

I came to the realization that if someone laughed at my dream, they were laughing at me. If they did not believe in me, I stopped associating with them. I had to. Because they had the power to make me doubt myself and, ultimately, quit.

After all, I was taking up the luge at the age of twenty-one; I was way too old. And I was trying to qualify for the Olympics just four years away. I could not leave anything to chance. I did not have time to waste. I needed to know right away who was "for" me and who was not.

How did I build my Dream Team? Simple; By telling everyone I spoke with about my dream. If they laughed at me, rolled their eyes, or in any way showed lack of belief, I stopped associating with them. I could not afford their disbelief to erode my self-belief. These were "dream stealers." In my mind, I thought, "You just watch me. I'll

159

make it happen." Once someone laughs at you, they should lose all influence over you, forever.

However, if they got excited about my dream, I held on to them like they were made of gold. That's how I found great encouragers for my Dream Team.

Most people will react to the pursuit of your dream in three stages: first, they will laugh at you; then, they will watch you; and, finally, they will begin to admire you. Don't listen to the dream stealers. Follow your heart.

People of integrity expect to be believed, and they're willing to let time prove them right.

Over time, I was able to find hundreds of supporters. An unexpected benefit in doing so was that I created a positive pressure which kept me from quitting when the going got tough. You see, no matter how rough a day I was having at the track, it was going to be easier to get back on the sled than to return home and tell everyone that I had quit.

That's how I found Tom. Believe me: you need some Toms in your life. You need to build your support network; your own personal Dream Team. The Toms of the world help you get through the struggle on the way to your victory.

Ninety percent of success is about the people you associate with. Winners will always encourage you and pull you up. Losers will do everything they can to pull you down.

Who you hang around with is entirely your choice. Birds of a feather flock together. Which flock are you in?

People always ask me, "What about if my family is negative? What do I do then?" Well, obviously, you can't disassociate yourself from your family. So if your family is negative, just don't talk to them about your dreams. If you do, you're asking for it. Just keep pursuing your dream and let your results speak for themselves.

Back to the story…

As soon as I put the phone down with the lady scheduling the Olympic Torch Run, I went across the street to share the good news with Tom.

"Hey Tom, guess what? I was just selected to carry the Olympic Torch when is goes across Kansas City in January!"

Tom was one of the few people who knew I was broke. He was one of the few that knew that I had maxed out my credit cards to fund my Olympic dream. As soon as Tom heard the good news, he pointed to his big van and said, "I'll drive you to Kansas City. Road trip!"

And that's exactly what Tom did. He drove me all the way from Houston to Kansas City and back. Twelve hours each way. He wouldn't even let me drive because he didn't want my arm to get tired. He said I needed to save my arm to carry the torch.

The streets of Kansas City were packed with a throng of people that had been waiting for hours to watch the Olympic Flame come by. They were all waving flags and shouting, "U-S-A! U-S-A! U-S-A!" It was awesome.

We rode in a special bus which dropped one of us off every quarter mile. As soon as they dropped me off and handed me the Torch, everyone on the street started cheering and shooting pictures like a bunch of paparazzi. Think of it: you're standing there, in the middle of the street, with a silly grin on your face, as you wait for the Torch to get to you.

The Torchbearer finally reached me, he lit my Torch, I gave him a high-five, and started my run. I could have covered my quarter mile in about a minute, but I "ran" this quarter mile in ten minutes flat. I ran it so slowly that I looked like a little old man. It didn't matter. I wanted to savor every step. It took me so long to cover my stretch that my arm started getting tired. I actually switched arms – I didn't want the next day's headlines to read, "Olympics Cancelled –

"I'll drive you to Kansas City. Road trip!" – Tom Duffy

Ruben Dropped the Torch."

Reaching the end of my leg, I lit the next runner's torch, and watched it for the longest time until it disappeared from my view. The next time I saw the Olympic Torch, I was sitting in the Opening Ceremonies of the Salt Lake City Olympics. All of my Olympic heroes carried it into the stadium – Scott Hamilton, Dorothy Hamill, Picabo Street, Dan Jansen, Bonnie Blair… it was incredible.

"Running" the Olympic Torch through Kansas City

As the torch was carried up the steps, everyone wondered who would get to light the huge Olympic Cauldron. The crowd went wild when they realized who had been chosen: the 1980 Lake Placid Miracle Hockey Team. The United States Olympic Committee chose the Miracle Team because they exemplified what the Olympics are all about. They were chosen because they believed when no one else believed.

It was all so perfect. The Miracle Team had helped inspire me to want to become an Olympic Athlete when they defeated the Soviets in 1980. Four years later, during my first time in Lake Placid I had stood right in the arena where it all happened. Finally, I was there, when they lit the Olympic Cauldron at the Salt Lake City Opening Ceremonies. It was the perfect ending of a dream come true.

"You always win by taking the journey. The journey transforms you. The person you become is the true purpose of the journey."

-Ruben Gonzalez

Putting it All Together
to Realize a Big Dream

It's funny how dreams are born. In February 2008 I was speaking at an event in San Diego. One of the other speakers told a story about a group of people who broke a Guinness World Record by building a house in under three hours. His story got me thinking about breaking world records. I had competed in the 1988 Calgary, 1992 Albertville, and 2002 Salt Lake City Olympics - three Olympics each in a different decade.

When I got home, I contacted the International Olympic Committee to find out if anyone had ever competed in four Olympics each in a different decade. They said it had never been done in the Winter Olympics.

That got me excited. It was February 2008 - 20 years to the month since I had competed in the 1988 Calgary Olympics as a 25 year old. The question was, could my old body still handle the brutal sport of luge? I had not taken a luge run in 6 years.

Well I decided to find out. When you get inspired by a dream you need to take action right away. Otherwise the excitement wears off, and you eventually regret your inaction.

Your Focus Determines
Your Experience

Before returning to the luge tracks, I called my good friend Jonathan Edwards, the U.S. luger who had helped fix my sled after my crash in Salt Lake City six years earlier.

I thought Jonathan might be able to give me some insights that would help me get over my fear of speed. By the way, if at this point you think it's ironic for a luger to be afraid of speed, I'm with you. In fact I could not agree with you more. I competed in the luge for years in spite of being afraid of the speed because the luge was my vehicle to the Olympics.

Focus on the action steps you need to take to reach your goal.

When I told Jonathan about my fear of speed, he said, "Ruben, you are focusing on the wrong thing. Luge is not about speed. Every luge track is fast. That's a given. You need to start focusing on what you need to be doing in each section of the curves. Focus on the steering and the fear will disappear."

It made sense. I was focusing on the circumstances – the speed. I needed to focus on the action steps that lead to a successful luge run – proper steering.

I went to the Salt Lake City track with renewed determination. I would focus 100% on my steering and 0% on the acceleration and speed. Incredibly, when I did, the fear disappeared. Overnight, simply by shifting my focus, the luge went from being an awful experience to being a fun and exhilarating ride. I felt more in control and more confident than ever before.

Note that it did not take me weeks, months or years to transform my fear into fun. The transformation occurred the moment I stopped focusing on my circumstances and started focusing on what I needed to do to succeed.

What about you? What are you focusing on at work or at home? Are you focusing on how challenging these recessionary times are or on how you can be the best that you can be? Are you focusing on how little you can do at work or how you can become the most valuable person at work? Market conditions and other people's attitudes are out of your control. Focus on what's the best thing you could do in the next 10 minutes to move your business forward.

Don't focus on the challenge. Focus on what you need to do to excel– at work, at home, in your relationships and in every other area of your life. When you do, you will immediately transform your experience and begin gaining confidence. You will start getting the best results in your life.

Fight for Your Dream

When I got home after my first enjoyable luge experience ever, I contacted the International Luge Federation (FIL) to find out what I needed to do to qualify for the Vancouver Olympics two years away. Their answer floored me. They said, "We won't let you slide in the World Cup Circuit. Number one, you're too old and number two, you've been away from the sport so long that if you get hurt, we'll look bad."

I told them, "You can't do that. At least give me a chance to prove myself."

They said, "The new Olympic track in Whistler, Canada is the fastest in the world. Up to now, only the Canadians have been training there. In a few weeks we will open the track for 10 days to allow the lugers from every other team to take 24 practice runs. Come to Whistler, take your 24 runs and afterwards we'll talk."

I went to Whistler. And he was right. The track was fast.

167

Really fast. Over 95 MPH (much faster than any other track). Everybody was crashing. Even the Olympic champion crashed. I didn't crash once. I didn't break any speed records, but I didn't break any bones either.

After the Whistler Test, the FIL (International Luge Federation) said, "Welcome back."

The FIL explained that in order to qualify for the Olympics I had to compete in five World Cup races over the 2008 and 2009 seasons and earn enough World Cup points to be in the top 40 in the world. I would have to learn new tracks and race people with ten times more experience than what I had. I decided to accept the challenge. After all, challenges are what make life exciting.

The next thing I did was to contact Ioan Apostol, the new coach of the FIL Team.

Back in 1988, the FIL realized that unless they took an active approach in developing luge around the world, luge would not remain an Olympic sport for long. At the time, the only countries with strong luge programs were Germany, Austria, Italy, and Russia. In 1988 the U.S. and Canada were just starting to get really serious about the sport of luge but were still not in the top level. The FIL decided to create a development team (the FIL Team) to help nations who did not have big luge programs in place. They bought a couple of vans, and hired Günther Lemmerer, my big Austrian coach. We were a ragtag team made up of athletes from countries like; Argentina, Brazil, Venezuela, Virgin Islands, Liechtenstein, Romania, Moldova, Slovenia, Korea, Taiwan, Hungary, Bulgaria, Spain, Tonga, New Zealand, Bermuda and a few more. We shared tools, shared knowledge, and shared anything that would give us a better chance when competing against the top teams.

From 1988 until 2002 I trained in the FIL Team under Günther Lemmerer. After 2002, Güenther was replaced by Ioan Apostol, a four time Olympian from Romania and

Robert Taleanu, a two time Romanian Olympian. Ioan and I had both competed in the Calgary and Albertville Olympics so we already knew each other.

When I contacted Ioan Apostol about joining the FIL Team, Ioan said, "Sorry Ruben, you have been away from luge too long. You can't be part of our team." I couldn't believe it. I had proven myself to the FIL but apparently that was not good enough for Ioan. Now I really didn't know what to do. I had no coach, nor could I afford to pay for a coach and fly him around the world.

When you have a dream you have to be prepared to fight for your dream. It will not be easy. Life will test you to see how serious you are. If you fight hard enough, the dream will reveal its secrets to you and you will find the way. But after Ioan turned me down, I was stumped.

There is Always a Way

Then my brother Marcelo, who had competed in Salt Lake City, came up with a great idea. Marcelo said, "You don't need a personal coach. There are coaches at every luge track. Make friends with them, explain your situation to them, and they will surely help you." Marcelo was right. Now I needed a game plan for the two pre-Olympic seasons and then I needed to start calling all the local luge coaches to build my "Olympic Qualification Multi Coach Support Team." Eventually I got help from the Georgian Luge Team* at the Latvian track, from Jonathan Edwards in Calgary, from Jon Owen in Salt Lake City, from Walter Corey in Whistler, and from the U.S. Team everywhere. If your attitude is that

* Nodar Kumaritashvili, who tragically died on the last training run of the 2010 Vancouver Olympics helped me out a lot. He showed me the best way to steer down the Latvian track while I was training there with the Georgian Team.

you will find a way to your dream no matter what, then life's challenges become only temporary inconveniences.

I called Jonathan Edwards so we could lay out a plan for the two seasons. The FIL required 5 races over the last two seasons but since I had been away from the sport so long, Jonathan decided that I needed to do more. The first season I would train and race in three races in order to start ramping up to world class level. On the second season I would race in four more races and hopefully would be able to make the cut. I sent my old sled to Salt Lake City for Jon Owen, one of the U.S. coaches to rebuild it for me (Jon and I had both competed in the 1988 Calgary Olympics). Time was not waiting for me so I had to take bold action.

Face Your Challenges

I've been a professional speaker since 2002. As a speaker I travel a lot. About once a week I hop on a plane to speak for corporations across America. But the speaking trips are usually one-nighters. Luge training trips were different. I was gone for weeks on end. I never traveled as much as I did when trying to qualify for Vancouver. Three trips to Europe, and three trips to Whistler, four trips to Salt Lake City and two trips to Calgary. And speaking in between whenever I had a few free days. Doing whatever it took to keep the dream alive.

The tracks we would be racing on complicated things. I had never even been to two of the tracks I had to race on – Lillehammer, Norway and Altenberg, Germany. So I needed to train at those tracks beforehand to figure them out. There was no room for error because the field was very competitive and only the top 40 in the world would get to compete in Vancouver. To say that competing in Vancouver would be a long shot was an understatement. But I had a big dream and a burning desire to realize it.

The thought processes that help you get to the Olympics are the same thought processes that will help you succeed in business and in life.

Successful people in all walks of life think big, focus on the possibilities, and take consistent bold action towards their objectives.

Some people tried to talk me out of it. These people said I had nothing to gain by making another Olympic team and that if I didn't make it would not look good - not for a professional speaker in the business of inspiring others to achieve more.

On the other end of the spectrum was a group of people that believed all I needed to do was to have a positive mental attitude and everything would just work out. I laughed, because PMA by itself will not do anything for you. You'll always have better results with a positive attitude than with a bad attitude, but PMA does not guarantee you'll win. PMA will keep you going when the going gets tough, but it does not guarantee you'll win.

When I told the PMA crowd that I thought my chances to qualify for Vancouver were 50/50, their jaws dropped and you could see their whole body slump with disappointment. I told them that if it was a sure thing, going for the Olympics would not be an adventure. I was after the adventure. I was after the challenge.

I raced in three World Cup races in the 2008 but my times were simply not competitive. Many people said I should give it up. I thought it would be crazy to quit. Quitting was simply not an option for me. I was too emotionally invested to quit. I figured that even if I didn't make it, the things I would learn about myself would make the struggle worthwhile.

I believe that in life you have to keep risking failure otherwise you atrophy. You have to always put yourself out on the line. You have to push your limits. You have to live

Coach Ioan, Coach Robert and I at the Olympics.

life to the fullest. Pushing your limits is how you learn more about yourself. Risking failure makes you dig deep inside and find out what you're really made of. That way, when life hits you with a storm, you know that you have what it takes to weather it.

My strategy was to do everything I could to position myself so that if some of the top guys messed up, I would somehow qualify (when I sold copiers I tried to be #2 with as many prospects as possible so that if their #1 copier guy messed up, I would be the guy they would call).

Something good came out of the 2008 season. Unbeknownst to me, coach Ioan Apostol of the FIL Team had been watching my progress and he invited me to be part of the FIL Team in the 2009 season - the season that led to the Vancouver Olympics in February 2010. That was great because now I would have much more coaching and experts working on my sled. Having personal coaches on the last season made a huge difference.

172

Be Proactive

Early in 2009 realized that unless I did something different I would keep getting the same results. So I had to do something different.

I had a couple of bad habits that were hurting my sliding times. The proper luge position is shoulders back, head back and feet pointed. Head back and feet pointed help you aerodynamically. Shoulders down help keep the sled stable and help you with steering. But it's hard to keep your shoulders and head down when you get into trouble in the track. As soon as you run into trouble, the knee-jerk reaction is to lift your head to see better. And as soon as you do that, your shoulders rise and you lose all stability. It's like if you were driving a car on the freeway, someone cut in front of you and your reaction was to take your hands off the steering wheel. It just doesn't make sense.

I had wrestled with this problem for twenty five years. All my coaches told me I needed to relax and put my shoulders back but they didn't tell me how to relax.

Knowing that I needed to do something to improve my times or else, I decided to call my good friend Don Akers. Don is an expert in how to condition your mind through the words you say to yourself.

Don spent a couple of hours with me. At one point he asked me what went through my mind when I got to a difficult section of the track. I told him that I always thought to myself, "Here it comes." Don got excited and said, "Here it comes? That's it! You're being reactive. By saying 'Here it comes.' You're mentally putting yourself at the mercy of the track. Saying 'Here it comes' is making you defensive and you will never be at your best if you are in a defensive state of mind."

"You need to say to yourself, 'Here I come!' 'Here I come' will make you proactive. It will help you attack the track and feel more in control. 'Here I come' will shift your thinking from victim mentality to victor mentality."

It made perfect sense. I actually wrote "Here I Come!" on top of my sled where I could see it before all my luge runs. And it started working. Slowly but surely, "Here I Come" helped me feel more relaxed and in control on the sled. My position started getting better and so were my times. The sport of luge starting to be fun because I felt more in control. I was no longer thinking "I hope I make it down." I started thinking, "I'm going to nail this run." And all of this started by simply changing what I said to myself.

Once I could control my sled better, coaches Ioan and Robert were able to do things to my sled that allowed me to go faster. We loosened the suspension and changed the shape of the steels to give me more speed.

Three months before the Olympics I still thought my chances were 50:50. But I kept training and making adjustments to my sled and slowly I started moving up in the standings.

Jump and the Net Will Appear

Three weeks before the Olympics I still didn't know if I was in. The qualification races were over and I was actually ranked 42 on the list at the time so technically I had not qualified for Vancouver. But I decided to continue training in Salt Lake City just in case something happened (you never know whether countries will send their athletes in or not).

For example, a couple of weeks before the 1988 Calgary Olympics, the top ranked luger got appendicitis and missed the games.

So even though I had not qualified for Vancouver, I planned to continue training just in case. You never give up until the final whistle is blown.

174

Jon Owen fixing my sled after a crash.

I had a couple of off days three weeks before the Olympics and on one of the days I was speaking to several hundred sales people in Minneapolis. I was telling them how you have to act boldly on your beliefs. Your actions show what you believe. You need to jump (take a chance) and the net will appear.

I told the salespeople how even though I still didn't know if I was going to the Olympics, earlier that day I had actually purchased non-refundable airline tickets to Vancouver for my wife, my kids and I. They looked at me like I was crazy. They probably thought I'd hit my head once too many in one of my luge crashes.

Well the next day I got the news. Norway decided not to send their three athletes because even though they were ranked in the top 40 in the world, it turns out that Norway only sends athletes that are in the top 20 in the World. With Norway out, I got bumped up to number 39 and I got to go.

The FIL Team before the Vancouver Olympic race.

I made it by the skin on my teeth – by a hair on my chinny-chin-chin. I jumped and the net did appear.

By not quitting when there seemed to be a very small chance of making it to the Olympics, by getting advice from the experts, and by doing things I had never done before, on February 12th, 2010, when I marched into the Opening Ceremonies of the Vancouver Olympics at the age of 47, I became the first person to compete in four Winter Olympics each in a different decade.

I was so happy that at the Opening Ceremonies I was about ready to carry the Norwegian flag!

How about you? What do you do when you're in a slump? What do you do when you get discouraged? What do you do when it looks like you will not reach your goals? Do you throw in the towel?

Sometimes it's OK to cut your losses and quit. Sometimes it's smart to quit. But don't quit right away. Think. Who's the top performing person you know that could possibly help

Gabriela and Gracen surprise me at the finish.

you get through your personal or professional minefield? Call them, meet with them and take advantage of their knowledge and experience. They may be able to come up with a game plan that will take you to the next level and let you shine.

It was great having my family at the Vancouver Olympics. On my last luge run Cheryl and our children Gabriela and Gracen surprised me as I was coming to a stop at the finish line. They were waiting for me at the grandstand. I reached out to touch them, the crowd went wild, and the photo of that moment is my most treasured souvenir from any of my four Olympics. It's the icing on the cake. It's my "Olympic Medal" at Last!

"The important thing in the Olympic Games is not to win but to take part, the important thing in life is not the triumph but the struggle. The essential thing is not to have conquered but to have fought well."

-Baron Pierre de Coubertin
Founder of the Modern Olympic Games

The Olympics are About the Dream

The Olympics are not about sports. The Olympics are about the Dream. They are just a place that showcases, to the world, the power of the human spirit. A place that shows people that, if you have a dream and you have the guts to go after it, and you refuse to quit – Dreams do come true.

Whenever you watch an athlete being interviewed during the Olympics, the word "dream" always comes up. Every athlete says the same thing, "It was always my dream."

Believe me, they don't tell us to say that. It just comes from the heart. What they do tell us is that, as Olympians, it is our responsibility to show others how we made our dream a reality. It is our responsibility to teach others how they, too, can make their Dreams come true because that is the best way we can make the world a better place.

"You gain strength, courage, and confidence by every experience in which you really stop to look fear in the face... The danger lies in refusing to face the fear, in not daring to come to grips with it... You must make yourself succeed every time. You must do the thing you think you cannot do."

- Eleanor Roosevelt

If I Could Do It,
You Can Do It

After reading my story, I hope you realize that there is nothing special about me. I'm just a plain guy who had a burning desire and was willing to do whatever it took, for as long as it took, to make it happen.

I just consistently and persistently followed success principles. Do yourself a favor: don't just read these principles. Apply them. Knowledge is not power. Applied knowledge is power.

I'm proof that these principles will work for anyone. After all, what are the chances that someone like me would go to the Olympics four times? I was just an average athlete, I did not take up my sport until the age of twenty-one, and to top it off, while living in hot and humid Houston, I picked a winter sport.

What were the odds? One in a million? One in ten million? I probably had a better chance to win the lottery.

I was just an ordinary kid with an extraordinary dream. I wasn't a big shot. I was a little shot that kept on shooting. Just like that young, scrappy U.S. Hockey Team that beat the mighty Russians. That's all they did. They believed in themselves and they just kept on shooting.

And that's something you can do too. If you start believing in yourself, you give it all you've got, and you refuse to quit, it will be just a matter of time before you make

Opening Ceremonies Salt Lake 2002

your dream come true, too; and just a matter of time before you start creating a better life.

Success is a choice. It's your choice. Make a decision that you will face your fears and do whatever it takes to get started. Make the decision to get off the stands and into the arena. Make the decision to stop existing and to start living.

Because if this little shot did what he did, then you can do anything.

Make the Decision to Stop Existing and to Start Living

PART FOUR

From Rags to Riches

2010 Vancouver Olympic Luge Ticket

"It's not whether you get knocked down. It's whether you get back up again."

- Vince Lombardi

How to Use
Success Principles
to Create a Better Life

This book is not about me. This book is about showing you how you can create a better life by consistently following some basic success principles. I want you to clearly see that the principles you've been reading about, will help you in every area of your life – at work, at home, in school, in the community, etc.

I can't think of a better way to do that than to share with you how I used these same principles to build a successful business. Owning your own business is not for everybody, but it had always been a dream of mine. When the opportunity for me to own my own business presented itself, I, of course, jumped on it.

I've been in sales all my life. Over the years I've sold all kinds of things: water coolers, cutlery, advertising, credit card terminals, mobile homes, insurance, etc.

For a few years I sold copiers in Downtown Houston. I have the dubious distinction of having cold-called every office in every floor of every building in Downtown Houston – twice. In order to keep my spirits up, I made a game out of it. I'd say to myself, "This is the only job where you get to start at the top – then I'd take the elevator to the top floor of a building and start cold-calling. By applying the law of averages, after a while I knew that based on my closing

187

average, every time I called on an office I made $20 whether they bought a copier or not. Knowing my closing average made it easier to call on many prospects every day.

Every top salesperson I have ever worked with had one thing in common. They invested in themselves. They realized that the better they were, the better their sales would be. Consequently, these top salespeople were constantly reading self-development books, listening to motivational and self-help audios, and attending success and sales seminars.

I did the same thing. I've always had an insatiable curiosity – an insatiable hunger for any bit of knowledge that would help me get better results. Over the years I've read hundreds of books and listened to thousands of audios on sales, management, leadership, customer service, negotiation, etc. I've sat through countless seminars. My attitude was that if I came away with just one good idea, it would be worth it. Because one good idea acted upon can change your life.

> *Invest in Yourself. The better you are, the better your results will be.*

You need to constantly invest in yourself too. In life you don't get what you want. You get what you are. If you want more, you need to get better. Tomorrow belongs to the people who are investing in themselves today.

About a month before the Salt Lake City Olympics something happened that changed my life. A fifth grade kid from my neighborhood came up to me and said, "Hey Ruben, when you get back from the Olympics, will you be my show-and-tell project at school?"

I told him, "Sure, sounds like fun."

After the Olympics, I went to his school, assuming that I would be speaking to a classroom of twenty-five to thirty students. Instead, the Principal walked me into the school's gymnasium filled with over two hundred kids – the whole fifth grade class was assembled. Show-and-tell for a classroom of kids had, somehow, turned into an assembly.

I wasn't necessarily nervous; just a little apprehensive. After all, I had never taken a speech class in my life. And, here I was, about to speak to over two hundred 11-year-olds for over forty-five minutes (a lot longer than I thought I would have to speak).

And then, something amazing happened: As I told the kids all of my Olympic stories, all the knowledge I had picked up from reading all those books, from listening to all those audios, and from going to all of those seminars, started pouring out of me. Half the time, I didn't know what the next thing out of my mouth would be. I just put it on autopilot and poured my heart out to them.

These kids heard forty-five minutes of funny Olympic stories illustrating the principles of success they would need to follow in order to succeed in life.

After the talk, as I was packing my things, a group of teachers surrounded me. Each face had a look of astonishment and they asked, "What do we have to do to get you to stick around for another hour? If you'll stay another hour, we'll pull the fourth graders out of class. They need to hear your story."

I told them, "Hey, that was kind of fun, bring 'em on!" In the end, my second speech was a little better than my first.

Afterwards, the Principal said, "Ruben, you have a gift. You're better than the speakers we pay. You need to do this for a living."

Well, I thought about it. Sharing my stories with those kids was a blast. I was being 100% myself. It felt effortless. And the teachers said my story was impacting the kids in a very positive way.

Everyone has a unique ability or area of brilliance; a gift; a talent that is so strong that is makes work seem effortless. Most of the time, it is something that seems so natural to us that we totally discount it.

That is why it is important to give a lot of weight to the compliments that others share with us because other people can usually see our unique talents better than we can.

Totally by chance, I had stumbled onto doing something which used my greatest talent: connecting with other people to inspire and equip them to be their best.

For three days, I thought about everything the teachers had said to me. They said I had a "gift." And, then, just like that, I quit my job. When I quit my job, we lost our heath insurance. Quitting my job was a huge risk because, at the time, our daughter Gabriela was only one year old, and Cheryl is a full time Mom so my income was our only income. My thinking was, "If I can sell a copier, I can sell myself as a professional speaker. I know I can make it happen and I will make it happen."

I burned my bridges. Burning my bridges forced me to commit 100% to making my new enterprise work. Burning my bridges put me in a position where it was going to be a "do or die" situation. Burning my bridges, instantly, created an urgency to get the job done – or else.

Since my first talk was at a school, I decided to call on other schools in Houston – over 700 of them – and market my motivational and inspirational keynote speech, "Becoming Unstoppable: Success Secrets of a Three-time Olympian." I made it a point to speak with the Principal, the counselor, and the President of the PTA. I wanted to create a buzz. I called the schools eight hours a day and, in the evenings, I followed up with faxes and emails. I was desperate. After all, I had to speak to eat.

God honors commitment. After a while the schools started calling back. Elementary schools, middle schools, high schools, colleges.

Speaking to assemblies ranging from five hundred to a thousand high school students is supposed to be a tough gig.

190

Being a big kid at heart, I did fine. My theory was that as long as I had fun and poured my heart out to them, they would have fun too. The teachers were amazed that I could hold their attention from forty-five minutes to an hour.

Business was great. I was working hard, marketing myself everywhere I went, and was completely focused; maybe a little too focused. Being so focused on calling on schools caused me to completely forget that the three summer vacation months would be totally dead months for me. I was so focused on schools that the thought of calling on corporations didn't even cross my mind.

The three summer months of 2002 were terrible. No speaking engagements. None. Both my family and Cheryl's family loaned us money to make ends meet, however, we eventually we dried out those resources, as well. Actually, it got to the point where we didn't want to keep asking for money.

We really had to tighten our belts. Figuratively speaking, it was macaroni and cheese time. Ramen noodles for dinner time. Things got so bad that we found ourselves three months behind on our mortgage. We almost lost the house.

Right in the middle of that desperate summer, I was offered a marketing job that paid more than I'd ever made selling copiers. After discussing it with Cheryl, we both agreed that if I took the job, it would just keep me from building a successful speaking business. It would derail me. It would take my focus away.

We decided to gut it out. We figured that if, somehow, we could make it through the summer, the business from schools would pick up in the fall. In the meantime, I would start focusing on breaking into the corporate and association markets.

By August, we could not even afford macaroni and cheese. At 6:45 AM on August 1st, 2002 I was outside the local welfare office about to sign us up for food stamps.

Only five months earlier, I had been at the top of the world – competing against the best in the world at the Salt Lake City Olympics. And now I was struggling – humbled by my circumstances.

As I stood outside the welfare office, waiting for them to open up at 7:00 AM, I heard the unmistakable sound of a small airplane flying overhead. I love flying airplanes.

"If you are going through hell......
Keep going!"
- Winston Churchill

I'm a private pilot with about 150 hours of flying time. Many years ago, I had "temporarily" given up flying to pursue my Olympic dream.

Seeing that Cessna flying overhead inspired me. I pulled out a business card and wrote on it, "It's August 1st, 2002. By August 1st, 2003 I will be debt free, own an Impreza (a new car) and will be flying again." Next time you're down remember: if you can look up, you can get up.

I believe God put that airplane up there for a reason; to remind me that I was down, but not out. That airplane reminded me that I was bound to succeed big because I was willing to put myself through the struggle. It reminded me that I was bigger than my circumstances and that I just needed to fight. Just like the people in all those biographies I had read about: Dream – Struggle – Victory. It's the only way.

We struggled through the summer. But we had hope in the future and were willing to do whatever it took to make it. When there is hope in the future there is power in the present.

We prayed like it was up to God and worked like it was up to us. And you know, we didn't pray for God to take the struggles away; that would have been the wrong prayer, because the struggles were there to make us stronger. We

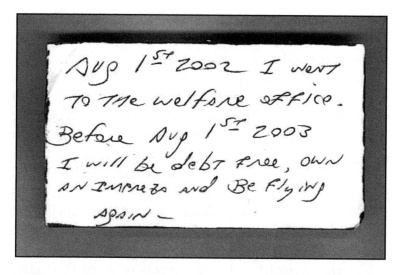

Aug 1st 2002 I went
To The welfare office.
Before Aug 1st 2003
I will be debt free, own
an Impreza and Be Flying
Again —

Don't ever lose hope. If you can look up, you can get up.

simply prayed for strength and wisdom. Sooner or later, you have to grow up; sooner or later, you have to stop telling God how big your challenges are and start telling your challenges how big God is. We prayed and we worked, because what you do shows what you believe.

Knowing I could not do it alone, I surrounded myself with winners and relied on their belief in me to get me through, just like I had done on the road to the Olympics. I started meeting some of the most successful speakers in Houston. I became a mentee to Jim Jacobus, a very successful Houston-based speaker. Jim taught me the speaking business.

One thing Jim would always tell me was, "Ruben, done is better than perfect. Perfectionists rarely succeed because they think too much and act too little. Get out there and work your rear end off and you can always clean up the mess later."

I followed Jim's advice. I called corporations and associations all day every day. Meanwhile, I spoke at just about every Rotary Club and networking club in Houston. The plan was to get as many people in Houston as possible to hear me speak in order to create a buzz and to create some momentum in my home market. Little by little, I started getting more and more corporate work.

My business was growing steadily, and then, about a year after that awful summer, the floodgates opened. All of a sudden, I started getting calls from businesses all over the United States with requests for me to speak for them. Businesses like Oracle, Xerox, Continental Airlines, Dell Computers, Wells Fargo, Coca-Cola, Shell Oil, and Johnson & Johnson started asking me to open and close their events or to be their sales kickoff speaker.

> *"A good plan, violently executed now, is better than a perfect plan next week."*
> *- General George S. Patton*

Every speaking engagement lead to others. It seemed that there was always someone in the audience that wanted me to speak for their group. To date, I've gotten to speak in 45 states and 13 countries - from Vietnam, to Singapore, to South Africa, to Switzerland, to Colombia, to Japan. Incredibly, only two years after being my young friend's "show-and-tell" project, I was sharing the stage with Zig Ziglar and Charlie "Tremendous" Jones, two of my heroes, in huge arenas all over the nation. That's not a "Ruben thing." That's a "God thing."

God honors commitment. There can be miracles if you believe and if you are willing to take massive action. But you have to be willing to go through the struggle if you want to taste the sweet taste of victory.

I see people everywhere seeking to live balanced lives. What they don't realize is that the only way to move up to another level, the only way to achieve their dreams, is to get temporarily unbalanced. You have to temporarily give things up to get to the next level. The faster you want to progress,

194

the more unbalanced you need to get. We wanted to get it done quickly and we were willing to make the necessary sacrifices. We were willing to follow the example of the people in the biographies.

How about you? Are you playing it safe? Are you holding back? Or are you going for it? Unless you are willing to go for it I guarantee you that you'll never succeed big. You have to be willing to fail big to win big.

I'm just an ordinary guy. I just followed some success principles. If I can do it you can do it. You are worthy of your dream. You were created to make it happen. It's your purpose in life. It's why you're here. Let yourself have it. If you don't dedicate your life to the pursuit of your dream, you'll

If you believe, and if you are willing to take massive action, miracles are possible.

be cheating yourself and you'll be cheating the world of your gifts.

There's dignity in being willing to fight - dignity in being willing to take the journey. Embrace the struggle. Learn to love the struggle because the struggle will make you great and will bring you closer to glory.

Do you have the courage to succeed? I believe you do. Go ahead. Burn those bridges. Go for the Gold. Make your life an adventure. It's the only way.

*"You have a choice to make.
You can get busy living,
or you can get busy dying."*

*- Andy Dufresne
"The Shawshank Redemption"*

Afterword

OK...you've read the book...now what?

Simply reading this book and putting it aside will make Ruben happy that you made a monetary investment in his future, but applying these principles in your daily life will make Ruben joyful that he was able to make a permanent investment in your future.

Assimilating information produces knowledge; and application produces wisdom, but only applying wisdom with courageous perseverance produces the fine pearls of success.

Too many people are buried under the gravity of a negative thought chain: problem... complaining... discouragement... self-pity... failure.

Those words look awful on paper, but they look ten times worse when they become part of someone's personal constitution.

Ruben's book, *The Courage to Succeed* confronts that negative thought process head-on with a positive thinking process: challenge... struggle... courage... action... success!

Those words look awesome on paper, but they look one hundred times better when they become part of your personal constitution.

Ruben Gonzalez is on a mission to encourage others towards success. Success does not just happen to people by accident. Success requires risk taking and risk taking requires traveling through some dark, threatening and seemingly deserted roads.

Reading *The Courage to Succeed* is like having Ruben as your personal torch-bearer. Ruben is able to illuminate some of the dark paths that can be intimidating and frightening when taking risks, but he cannot make success happen for you. Nobody can do it for you. Ruben provides a light for the path but you must do the running. You must have the courage to persevere. And Ruben will be cheering you all the way to the finish line.

Ruben has been on a lifelong search for clues that lead to success. He's been on his search with a magnifying glass in one hand and a torch in the other. Now he is inviting us along with him to blaze a trail of success and legacy. This book should not be read once and shelved. Find a magnifying glass, search the depths of this book over and over again, and discover an inexhaustible treasure that will enrich every area of your life. Then, light your torch from Ruben's and begin to passionately inspire and encourage others to live their lives with a steadfast spirit of integrity and personal resolve.

P.S. – Then go and write a book about it and share it with the rest of us!

George A. Palombo

Executive Director - American Center
for Character and Cultural Education
2001 Pennsylvania Police Officer of the Year

Ruben's Rules for Success

1. You will never achieve anything great in life until you start believing that something inside you is bigger than the circumstances you face.

2. You can become great by making a decision to pursue your dream in life and by refusing to quit.

3. Every success you've ever had or will ever have is the product of your courage to act and the courage to endure.

4. Success is not about how much talent you have. It's about what you do with the talent you do have.

5. Successful people love the battle, the challenge and the journey. It's about knowing that you did your best.

6. If you do whatever it takes for however long it takes, success is only a matter of time.

Reading List for Winners

As a Man Thinketh
 - James Allen

Success! The Glen Bland Method
- Glenn Bland

The Power of Focus
- Jack Canfield and Mark Victor Hansen

How to Win Friends and Influence People
-Dale Carnegie

Man's Search for Meaning
- Viktor Frankl

How to Have Power and Confidence in Dealing with People
-Les Giblin

Think & Grow Rich
 - Napoleon Hill

Life is Tremendous
 - Charlie Jones

See You at the Top
-Zig Ziglar

The Power of Positive Thinking
- Norman Vincent Peale

Tough Times Never Last but Tough People Do
- Robert Schuller

Slaying the Dragon
- Michael Johnson

Create Your Own Future
-Brian Tracy

Seeds of Greatness
-Dennis Waitley

Simple Steps to Impossible Dreams
- Kevin Scott

Winning Every Day
- Lou Holtz

Rhinoceros Success
- Scott Alexander

They Call Me Coach
- John Wooden

The Dip
- Seth Godin

The Traveler's Gift
- Andy Andrews

Dare to Win
 - Mark Victor Hansen and Jack Canfield

The Magic of Thinking Big
- David Schwartz

The Aladdin Factor
- Jack Canfield and Mark Victor Hansen

The Slight Edge
- Jeff Olson

How to Be Like Mike
- Pat Williams

Finding the Champion Within
- Bruce Jenner

The Speed of Trust
- Stephen Covey

Pushing the Envelope
- Harvey Mackay

How to be Like Walt
- Pat Williams

The Success Principles
- Jack Canfield

Developing the Leader Within
- John Maxwell

Bounce
- Matthew Syed

Recommended Biographies

Success leaves clues. Reading the lives of people who have accomplished great things helps develop belief, and shows us what works and does not work in life.

In fact, in the olden days, reading biographies was part of people's education. People like Abraham Lincoln, George Washington, and Thomas Jefferson learned their leadership skills by reading biographies.

At home, my wife Cheryl and I regularly read biographies to our daughter Gabriela and our son Gracen. Gabriela and Gracen are learning the great thoughts of great people. Our finished product is their raw material. Imagine what they will accomplish in 20 years.

Cheryl Reading to the Kids...

**The lives and stories of these people have had
a profound impact on my life:**

George Patton
George Washington
Wilma Rudolph
Ronald Reagan
Abraham Lincoln
Nelson Mandela
Viktor Frankl
John Adams
Walt Disney
Andrew Carnegie
Winston Churchill
Benjamin Disraeli
Mohandas Gandhi
Thomas Edison
Albert Einstein
Ray Kroc
Harlan Sanders
John Wooden
Henry Ford
Mario Andretti
Donald Trump
Robert E. Lee
Martin Luther King
Mother Theresa
Benjamin Franklin

Inspirational Movies

Success requires massive action. These movies will inspire you to start taking action towards your dreams.

Rudy

Rocky

Miracle

Iron Will

Apollo 13

Gladiator

The Rookie

Braveheart

Cool Runnings

The Right Stuff

Chariots of Fire

16 Days of Glory

Slumdog Millionaire

The Shawshank Redemption

The Champion's Creed

Read this every morning with passion and you are guaranteed to have a better and more productive day.

I am a champion.

I believe in myself.

I have the will to win.

I set high goals for myself.

I have courage. I never give up.

I surround myself with winners.

I'm cool, positive, and confident.

I'm willing to pay the price of success.

I love the struggle and the competition.

I stay relaxed and in control at all times.

I focus all my energy on the job at hand.

I vividly imagine that victory will feel like.

I am a champion and I <u>will</u> win.

For a free copy visit
www.TheChampionsCreed.com

My Creed

by Dean Alfange

I do not choose to be a common man. It is my right to be uncommon. I seek opportunity to develop whatever talents God gave me. I do not wish to be a kept citizen, humbled and dulled by having others look after me. I want to take the calculated risk; to dream and to build, to fail and to succeed. I refuse to barter incentive for a dole. I prefer the challenges of life to the guaranteed existence; the thrill of fulfillment to the stale calm of utopia. I will not trade freedom for beneficence nor my dignity for a hand out.

I will never cower before any earthly master nor bend to any threat. It is my heritage to stand erect, proud, and unafraid; to think and act for myself; enjoy the benefits of my creations and to face the world boldly and say – "This, with God's help, I have done."

"Success is like wrestling a gorilla You don't quit when you're tired. You quit when the gorilla is tired!"

- Robert Strauss

About the Author

Ruben Gonzalez wasn't a gifted athlete. He didn't take up the sport of luge until he was 21. Against all odds, four years, and a few broken bones later, he was competing in the Calgary Winter Olympics. At the age of 47 he was racing against 20-year-olds in the Vancouver Olympics.

As a Four-Time Olympian, peak-performance expert and business author Ruben Gonzalez knows how to achieve success again and again.

As a master storyteller and keynote speaker, Ruben uses his Olympic experiences to inspire audiences to think differently, live life with passion and have the courage to take the necessary steps toward their goals – to push beyond self-imposed limitations and to produce better results.

Ruben's appeared nationally on ABC, CBS, NBC and FOX. He's been featured in Time Magazine, BusinessWeek, The New York Times as well as publications in all over the world. His articles on peak-performance are read in every continent.

His clients include, Xerox, Oracle, Coca-Cola, Microsoft, Oracle, Shell Oil, United Airlines, Farmers Insurance, Johnson & Johnson, Ortho McNeal, Blue Cross Blue Shield, Wells Fargo, RE/MAX, New York Life, The U.S. Treasury Department and many more.

Ruben lives in Colorado with his wife Cheryl and their children Gabriela and Gracen. He enjoys the challenge of climbing Colorado's fourteen-thousand-foot peaks, snowboarding, sailing and flying.

Join the Thousands of high achievers who have learned how to become unstoppable on the way to success.

Sign up for Ruben's Monthly Success Tips.

To subscribe visit:
FourWinterGames.com

Book Ruben for Your Next Event

To have Ruben speak to your organization or to order any of his other personal and professional development products call:

832-689-8282
FourWinterGames.com